WHERE'S THE PARTY?

Lessons in Drug Prevention:
Handbook Three
The How-To Party Protocol
Book for Parents and Teens

D0977666

By
Miles To Go
Kelly Townsend, M.S. & Jonathan Scott

Where's The Party?
Lessons in Drug Prevention: Handbook Three
The How-To Party Protocol Book for Parents and Teens
First Edition

To order additional copies, visit www.milestogodrugeducation.com
Kelly Townsend, M.S. & Jonathan Scott

This book was developed from the parent lecture of the same name created by Miles To Go for their Drug Abuse Prevention Lecture Series. Miles To Go is based in Southern California.

The material contained in this book is meant to provide the reader with information for drug abuse prevention purposes only. It is not a substitute for medical advice, diagnosis or treatment. Contact a medical professional immediately in cases of substance abuse and possible overdose.

While the authors have made every effort to provide accurate information and internet addresses at the time of publication, neither the publisher nor the authors assume any responsibility for errors or changes that occur after publication.

ISBN: 978-1480057111

1

Dedication

To Z. and her peers.

Special Thanks

We want to extend a special thank you to our editor, Jan Williams, who drops everything to edit our books. The job is huge, and her efforts dwarf our heartfelt thanks.

Table of Contents

Part 1

The Challenge

Answering the Big Questions

1.1 Most of us survived parties in high school. Aren't parties a rite of passage?

This is a book about teen parties—not the ones where a few pizzas get ordered or where close friends gather in search of a good movie. No, this is a book about the other teenage parties— the ones where adults look the other way as teens drink and use drugs; or where kids wait until their parents go away for the weekend and then stage an epic bash. As you read the paper or scanned the Internet in the year or so before this book was published, you may have seen a number of headlines about the latter kind of party. If you did not see the reports we are talking about, we'll recap a few for you:

- In March of 2012 in Salt Lake City, Utah, a 16-year-old girl tried to mimic a fictional party portrayed in a movie released earlier that month. Instead of a few friends, though, she ended up with over 100 strangers in her parent's home; and one of those strangers was a gang member who proceeded to open fire. The girl was shot in the foot, but three other partygoers were more seriously wounded—one was shot in the back, another in the neck, and the third had a bullet graze his head.

• In August of 2012, a 19-year-old female fell from a moving party bus onto a highway in Minnesota. Amazingly, she survived. A little less amazing was the way her friends responded—not one of them lifted a finger to dial 911 for fear they would be held accountable for their underage drinking. It took them 20 minutes to get around to telling the bus driver about the missing passenger. By the time police arrived, reports indicate that only 11 of the 35 teens could be located; the rest had scattered in an effort to avoid getting into trouble.

• On July 14, 2011, ABC News reported the alcohol overdose death of a 14-year-old girl at her own slumber party.

• On March 3, 2012, a 17-year-old from Panorama City, CA, died during the night from an overdose of alcohol he consumed at a binge-drinking party the night before. The young man's mother was concerned when her son failed to come home; and she found his body in a bed at a friend's house where he went to sleep it off.

These tragic examples are just the surface manifestations of the costs teenage drug and alcohol use extract from us as individuals, families, and communities. Sadly, the real damage caused by this type of behavior by teens at parties waits for us well down the road. As you make your way through this book, you will learn that adolescents exposed to drug and alcohol use during that period of their lives are courting nothing less than disaster. This devastation comes in the form of increased rates of drug abuse, dependence, and addiction; in alcoholism and alcohol abuse; in cognitive difficulties; in mental illness; in violence and sexual abuse; in learning impairments; in car accidents and DUI's; in increased disease rates and health problems; in emotional dysfunction and impairment; in the loss of opportunity and freedom; in domestic issues and divorce; and in the destruction of the relationships between children and their parents.

It is tempting to see the litany above as overkill. Audience members frequently approach us after parent presentations to describe how they drank and used drugs when they were young and wonder aloud how it is that they turned out fine. While we certainly do not feel it is appropriate for us to argue with them about the definition of 'fine', we do know this: in the past, a common way to judge the effects drugs and alcohol had on a particular life was to rely on anecdote. Most of the reports about the perceived costs associated with teen drug and alcohol use came directly from those who used them, and that measurement system is the very definition of unreliable.

Today, much of what is known about how drugs and alcohol negatively impact teens comes from peer-reviewed scientific studies and from imaging techniques that allow us to observe (often in real time) what happens to drugged brains. The confusing part about drug and alcohol use by teens is that it destroys some of them while others seem to get away with it completely. We are not trying to tell you that if you drank or did drugs when you were young that you have effectively been destroyed; but we are saying that teen drug and alcohol use always comes with a price—even if that price isn't immediately obvious.

It is time for us to stop paying these invisible costs. The news stories and issues listed above are very real, and they are rooted in teen drug and alcohol use. We will show that the majority of that use happens at teen parties; and we will plead the case that until we learn how to manage the ways our children socialize with each other in large groups we will continue to bear the burdens associated with this behavior. We want this above all else to be clear: we pay this debt with the futures and the lives of our children.

We must keep in mind that parties are not the cause of all this death, destruction, and heartbreak; it is the alcohol and drugs consumed by the teenage participants that bring about the terrible events described. Therefore, this is a book *about* parties, but it is not a book *against* parties. Instead, it focuses on how you can go about making sure your child's parties do not include drugs and alcohol as a part of the picture.

If you are to realize this goal, the first requirement is that you establish healthy relationships and open lines of communication with your children. While a good part of this book is devoted to actions you can take that directly pertain to parties, the sections that discuss brain development and social challenges are no less important. The ideas they highlight are at the center your efforts to build healthy relationships with your children.

1.2   How do we know if we are making good parenting choices?

Parents are the last line of defense when it comes to the dangers parties pose for their children, but many find themselves trying to do a job they are ill equipped and ill prepared for. It is critical for parents to improve their skills.

One of the most important aspects of this discussion relates to the style of parenting shown to be most effective when dealing with teens. Terms commonly used when discussing parenting styles include permissive, authoritarian, and authoritative.

Permissive parents are rarely troubled when their children use drugs and alcohol at parties; and they rarely expend lots of energy arguing with their kids about right and wrong. Permissive, laissez-faire parents are OK with almost everything, and they may not even bother to ask what their children's plans are for the evening.

Unfortunately, it is a false sense of security they enjoy. Children of permissive parents regularly report feeling less valued and protected than children of parents who take the time to discuss and institute boundaries. Further, these children gain little comfort from parents who are more concerned with what their kids want than what they need. Sadly, when it comes to drug and alcohol use rates, a 2010 Brigham Young University (BYU) study reported that indulgent parents—who rated low in accountability and high in warmth—almost tripled the likelihood their children would drink heavily.

At the other end of the spectrum are the authoritarian parents who insist on blind, unquestioning adherence to a stated set of rules. The authoritarian is very much about right and wrong, black and white. The children of parents who act this way often feel untrustworthy and incapable of choosing the correct path on their own. As they grow older, many feel the need to chafe against their bonds and rebel against the overbearing authority figure; others simply submit and accept that they cannot be trusted, only controlled. Either way, the children of authoritarian parents rarely learn how to self-regulate or make decisions based on their own sense of right and wrong. These parents are referred to in the BYU study as high in accountability but low in warmth; and their outcomes are almost as bad as the permissive parents' are. Children of authoritarian parents are more than twice as likely to drink heavily.

Authoritative parents manage to walk the middle ground—they have high expectations of accountability and yet they manage to combine those with a high level of warmth and regard for the abilities and character of their children. They rarely find themselves insisting things must be just so, but they do spend large amounts of time and effort finding out who their children are, what they are involved in, what they think, and what they need to successfully navigate their environments. Authoritative parents understand that their children have to make mistakes in order to learn, but they are present when the mistakes those children make become dangerous or life threatening. They are willing to step in when necessary, even if it might be uncomfortable or embarrassing in the short term.

When accountability and warmth are both high, children get the message that they are protected but not controlled, and the results are the reward—children of these parents are the least likely to drink heavily. Additionally, a recent study showed that children raised by authoritative parents were much less likely to abuse alcohol even after leaving home to attend college.

In fact, authoritative parents can have positive effects that extend beyond their own children. In late 2012, a study showed that the friends of teens with authoritative mothers were much less likely to get drunk, binge drink, smoke cigarettes, and smoke marijuana. Authoritative parents do not just affect their own families; their influence benefits the entire community.

The challenge is how to be an authoritative parent when it comes to teen parties. While there will never be a one-size-fits-all solution, there are guidelines that can help establish a base from which to operate. While it is illogical to imagine that teens will encourage their parents to institute guidelines and expectations, they desperately need parents who are willing to play the unpopular role of overseer.

The first expectation that has to be established is that drugs and alcohol are off-limits. You should not see this as a way to control your child, but rather as a statement of concern regarding safety. It is not about right vs. wrong, it is about healthy and safe vs. dangerous and deadly.

Not using is not enough, though. You must also make it clear that your children must not remain in the presence of other kids who are using. This has to include a prohibition against ever getting in a car with anyone who has been drinking or getting high—even if that person is not driving. Drunken teens will do all kinds of dumb things in a car, and that includes interfering with the ability of the driver to drive safely.

Telling your children they are not allowed to go to drug and alcohol parties doesn't mean they will never be able to do anything fun or social (despite what they believe at the time). It does mean that parents have to educate themselves about how to ensure the parties their children want to attend are going to be safe.

1.3 How can I help my teen deal with parties when he won't even listen to me?

For much of recorded history adults have looked upon teenagers as a problem they had to tolerate; a thorn in their collective sides that they could not remove. Today, we have a new perspective on teenagers and their brains. This new view lets us see that while teenagers may drive us up the wall with skill and frequency, they do not usually do so intentionally. When we look at our children as they grow into adolescence and young adulthood, it's tempting to nostalgically look back at the way they were when they were little—often sweet, certainly innocent, but most of all, easier to handle.

When children enter their teens, we cannot afford to hold on to the people they were when they were very young. It is OK to reminisce, but today you have to deal with this new person in your life—your teenage son or daughter. Try to remember that this can be a confusing time for them as well. They often feel as though a stranger is looking back at them from the mirror; and they have to negotiate this new existence with little or no information on how to do that. They are experiencing feelings they have never felt before; their bodies are changing in ways that can make them feel both self-conscious and wildly powerful at the exact same instant; and they are forced to navigate an increasingly complex world while feeling utterly confused and in over their heads.

The most critical thing to remember is that they are not adults, even if they look like they are. Science now tells us that the son who is six inches taller than you are—while he might be physically mature and intimidating—is working with a brain that is still years away from full function. When confronted by complex decisions, his pre-frontal cortex is barely making do and he can frequently find himself completely overwhelmed by temptation and impulse.

We have to remember that we do not do our kids any favors when we try to exert absolute control over their behavior. Only by actually making decisions will they strengthen the connections in their brains needed for decision-making; and they will only understand the consequences of their actions if they experience the costs associated with their decisions. Our job is to help them as much as we can (and as much as they will let us). We may have lost absolute control, but we have not lost the power to be good influences and good role models in our kids' lives. We may no longer be able to declare the best way to do things; but we can offer suggestions and ask questions about possible consequences as our kids venture farther afield.

It is of the utmost importance that we clearly and regularly outline our expectations, rules, and consequences with our children. We cannot fall prey to the impression that what we say does not matter; even when our children show every sign that they are actively ignoring everything we say. Kids seem to have the amazing ability to recall something they do not even appear to have heard.

This is not just about having teenagers do what we want; it's about helping them manage real situations they are likely to find themselves in—like parties. They may not always make the right choices and control their impulses, but they must be able to practice making moral decisions within the framework of a clear set of rules and expectations. As they get more practice, the neural network they use to make decisions in the face of temptation and impulse will increase in ability and efficiency.

On occasion, we may find ourselves deeply troubled by our children's actions—how they treat us, how they speak to us, how they function out in the world. It is normal in situations like these to feel distressed, but the one thing science shows us is that we should never lose hope. The brain of that troubling child is changing on a minute-to-minute basis, and that means we can never give up. What presents as a problem child today may be tomorrow's superstar, or simply tomorrow's good kid. Both are equally wondrous outcomes.

When you are having a tough time understanding the way your teen is acting, try to think back to a time when he or she had difficulty handling something at the age of two or three—it's probably not the problem now that it was then. Your teen no longer acts as he or she did at two or three for a very specific reason—he or she grew out of it. As it matures, a child's brain develops new abilities and gains new skills. The same thing is going to happen now, if you give it a chance; and if you lend a hand or intercede only when you see the real potential for harm.

We are not saying that this is the time for you to kick back and let the chips fall where they may—far from it. In fact, we think now is the time you have to up your game. The role you play now will be more complex and more important than ever. Some kids are going to decide it is a good idea to drink, others will think it is OK to smoke some marijuana, and many will think it is time they be allowed to go to parties where all of these things are happening. It is not time; and it never will be while they are teenagers. Parents of teenagers have to be extra vigilant, because teens have so few skills when it comes to making good decisions and yet they live in a world of ever-increasing risk. Teens today can get into a lot more trouble simply by virtue of the larger menu of options from which they can now choose.

Understanding your teen's brain allows you to have new insight into and empathy for what he or she is going through. You will always love your children, but it is so much easier to like them when you see them less as adversaries and antagonists and more as unskilled, unpracticed teens navigating one of the most trying and confusing stages of life. It pays to remember that your teens either barely understand or, more likely, are as confused by their behaviors as you are. Try to have a thick skin as you raise your teens. It is a decision that is so much more proactive and shows so much more promise than does lowering yourself to your teenager's skill level when they say or do something offensive.

Science has given us the power to make new, more informed choices when it comes to how we parent these little brain factories we have living under our roofs. The opportunity awaits. If we want the best out of our children, we owe them nothing less than our best; and that means we must take the time and make the effort to learn as much as we can about how their brains work and what challenges they face in their daily lives. If you take the concepts and suggestions outlined in this book and apply them in your interactions with your teenager, you have taken a big step down that path.

1.4 The other parents are serving alcohol to teens at parties. Am I the only one who isn't?

Unfortunately, this is one of the situations where you can find yourself the victim of peer pressure from other parents. There are two different scenarios where you can find yourself at odds with or unsupported by other parents when it comes to parties.

The first is the most troubling and most obvious: some parents think teens are going to use drugs and alcohol no matter what we do. They think we should either turn a blind eye or just completely give up and party with them. We want to say again that these options are unsafe, unhealthy, and irresponsible. Teens cannot use drugs of abuse or alcohol legally or safely; so it is self-defeating when we assume they will, damaging when we condone it, and against the law when we participate in their use.

The second situation is more a case of parental paralysis or resting inertia. These parents don't really think it's a good idea for their children to be drinking or using drugs, but they see so many other parents allowing it or that appear unaware it is happening that they don't see how they can be the only ones who say no. They cannot figure out how to make the point that it is unsafe for their child to do what so many other parents appear to be OK with their children doing. Your teen will gladly point this out to you, and they will be more than willing to make the general statement that you are the only parent in the whole world who will not let their kid be normal and have fun.

This is the unfortunate truth for many parents: they feel completely alone in their belief that teens should not be drinking and using drugs when they socialize with their friends. In fact, while it may be true that they feel alone, it is not a reality. They just think they are alone because the other parents who feel the same way have not spoken out either. In the face of this deafening silence, many parents operate on the assumption that the group believes that teen drug and alcohol use is unavoidable and uncontrollable; and if these parents want to fit in, they will follow the group. In this case, that will require they do nothing; but doing nothing is the last thing their child needs them to do—he or she needs them to step up.

This is a perfect example of what we must do as parents if we want our kids to deal well with peer pressure—we have to show them how. It is our duty to stand up for what we believe, even if we think we are alone. Eventually, if enough people do this, there will come a time when what was once unpopular will become the norm—parents will realize that they are not the only ones who don't want their kid to drink or do drugs at parties; they are actually members of a no-longer-silent majority. In order for this to happen, more people have to speak out in support of the idea that teenage parties should not feature drug and alcohol use. It is our hope that this book can play the role of catalyst for these parents. Once they understand they are not alone, they will be inspired to act.

1.5 What is the best piece of advice you can give parents?

Children who have strong relationships with their parents are less likely to be the victims of undesirable peer influence. Therefore, parents can be a vaccine against the infection of peer pressure. We always advise parents to interact with their children after they return from a night of socializing with their friends, but it is also important for you to greet them earnestly each time they return home or when you see them after a period of absence.

We are frequently amazed and troubled by the behaviors exhibited by parents and students during the afternoon pick-up. In most of the schools we work with bus service is limited or nonexistent, so parents pick their children up after school. Often, this is what we see: The parent pulls up and stops. The child walks to the car, opens the door, tosses in his or her backpack, then follows the backpack into the car and closes the door. Sometimes not a word passes between the parent and child the entire time.

It is certainly possible that animated and earnest greetings pass between them after they pull out, but it seems to us that some of the passion of the hello is lost if it is not said until many minutes have passed since the reconnection. It is also possible that things do not improve after they pull away together; that parent and child sit in a state of stony silence for the entire ride home. For whatever reason, both parent and child have lost an opportunity to indicate that they missed each other and that the reconnection means a lot to both of them.

While it may be understandable for a teen to want to maintain the façade of coolness while his or her friends are watching, we owe it to our children to greet them enthusiastically when we reconnect. It is our way of saying to them, "I really missed you. I'm glad to see you." Our kids need to know, and be reminded, that we like them, love them, and miss them when they are gone. Do not expect this effort to be encouraged by your children directly, but don't let their demeanor trick you into thinking that they don't value it when it happens. One of the major jobs our children are working on in adolescence is who they will ultimately become. The last thing you want to do is leave this job up to your child and his peers, and yet it seems this is exactly what they want to happen. It is up to us to make sure it does not.

We think you will gain a lot of passion for the job of parenting if you just keep repeating in the back of your mind, "If I don't do it, his friends will." We do our children a disservice when we buy into the idea that they do not need our love and positive regard as they get older. In fact, they may need it more as they grow older, and if we deprive them of our connection as they age, they will be more likely to seek that connection through their peers.

1.6 I keep hearing about social host laws—what are they?

Only recently have most states considered or enacted legislation that specifically prohibits adults from directly providing alcohol to teens or knowingly allowing its use by underage partygoers. In the past, the police had to rely upon laws that pertained to contributing to the delinquency of a minor when they wanted to address the issue of adults allowing the use of alcohol by teens. Today, a number of states and municipalities are considering or have passed legislation that specifically prohibits adults from allowing or encouraging the use of alcohol by underage drinkers at parties. These laws are referred to as *social host laws*.

As of January 1, 2011, disappointingly few states had social host laws on the books. A number of those failed to include penalties that addressed the issue of adults allowing the illegal use of alcohol to occur in their presence in cases where the adults did not directly provide the alcohol used. States like Delaware have recently taken steps to address this blind spot.

Some states, including California, have no social host laws that carry legal consequences; but instead have laws that provide for civil penalties or financial consequences for damages or injuries that result from underage drinking that occurs on an adult's watch.

We hope that as more states introduce social host legislation fewer adults will be motivated to allow the use of alcohol by teenagers and underage drinkers. This change in the law will ultimately result in a new consciousness—one that treats teen alcohol use as the social and health issue it is. It has been too long in coming, but we applaud its arrival.

Due to the dynamic changes occurring in the field of social host laws, any outline of current legislation presented here would be out-of-date almost overnight. For that reason, we will create a page on our website so you will be able to find current information on this important topic. We invite you to follow social host law developments by visiting our site at www.milestogodrugeducation.com.

1.7 How can we help our kids attend and host parties safely?

This book is going to help you deal with the issue of teen parties in ways that are positive, effective, and based in science. Our goal is to make sure that by the time you finish reading you will have the knowledge, the techniques, and the confidence to help your child manage the challenges parties present.

This book is laid out so that you can start today to prepare yourself and your child for the impending parties in your lives. The hands-on techniques in Part 2 will detail exactly how to go about allowing your teen to attend or host a party. It will cover the steps to take when your teen wants to attend a party; what to do in the weeks leading up to a party your child wants to host; what to do the day of your child's party; and some basic steps to take if you're leaving town but your teenager is staying behind.

Part 3 deals with how to go about using consequences when your teen behaves in a manner that requires guidance or correction. While the information in this section is useful if your teen makes a bad decision at a party, it also applies in other areas where teens are likely to make mistakes as well.

Part 4 addresses the issue of peer pressure in your child's life; first in how to define and understand it, then in how to mitigate its effects.

Part 5 delves into your teen's brain. We feel that if you have a basic but clear picture of how your child's brain is changing and operating, you will be better able to parent in ways that increase the quality of the communication that passes between you and the depth of the relationship you share. This section outlines some of the most important concepts you need if you want to understand your teen's behaviors.

Part 6 addresses the direct threats posed by drug and alcohol use by teens. In it, we will break down the dangers and risks by topic—we will discuss both immediate and the long-term repercussions as they relate to alcohol, street drugs, and prescription drug abuse. We will also highlight the risks associated with increased violence and sexual activity (both consensual and assaultive) that make teen parties so infamous.

In Part 7 will pull together all the ideas and challenges we have discussed; and we will also review the issues parents must deal with if they want their children to be both socially skilled and physically and emotionally safe.

So, if you're ready—let's get started!

Part 2

The Party: What To Do

2.1 When Your Children Go To Parties

• *The Cardinal Rule*: When your children attend parties, you should occasionally make it a point to check on them at random. It is your responsibility as a parent to monitor the way your child socializes, and to be sure that your notion of what is going on matches the reality of what is going on. There is a critical lack of parental oversight when it comes to party behavior. The most common drug and alcohol use environment for teens is at parties, and yet it is the least likely place for parents to be active and present. In order for parties to change, this must change first.

• Your children have to provide you with the names and phone number of the parents of the child hosting the party. No contact information—no party.

• You have to get in touch with the host's parents, and get assurances from them that they will be present and actively chaperoning the party. These include:

1. Do they know about the party?

2. What are the party parameters—start time, end time, location, theme, etc.?

3. How many people do they expect to attend? Is this an open party, or will a limited number of guests be invited?

4. Will alcohol and drugs (including tobacco) be forbidden?

5. Will they have a one entry per person policy? If a partygoer leaves, will re-entry be barred?

6. Will there be an adequate number of adults to oversee the number of attendees?

7. What are the parents' plans if things go awry—if someone shows up with alcohol, under the influence, or the party gets out of control?

These questions are hard to ask, but you have to ask them. If the host's parents react negatively or evasively, it may signal a problem.

- When you drop your child off, make it a point to introduce yourself to the host's parents. If you cannot find them or if you see that there is no adult oversight present, it is time to take your child back home or out to a different activity. If adults are present but something feels wrong or the circumstances seem inappropriate (the adults are drunk, lots of alcohol is present and unsupervised), do not let your child stay. Trust your instincts and impressions. Remember, it is your child's job to tell you how

24

wrong you are, but he or she is often secretly relieved when you do your job and keep him or her out of harm's way. You can do this in such a way as to not embarrass your teen in front of his or her peers. Have your child check back with you ten or fifteen minutes after you arrive at the party. If what you see makes you uncomfortable, you can leave first and have your teen follow a few minutes later. This allows him or her to save face by not having to be led out of the party by mom or dad. If your teen fails to reconnect with you at the appointed time—or fails to follow your exit from the party—you are now free to go find him or her. Any embarrassment that results is because of your teen's failure to follow the agreed upon script, and you should point this out if any complaining ensues.

• Provide your phone number to the host's parents, and encourage them to call if they have any issues or concerns.

• Reiterate to your children your feelings about drug and alcohol use. Be very clear about why using them is dangerous and unhealthy. This requires, at a minimum, fluency in the risks cited in Part 6 of this book. Be consistent with your limits—you cannot serve alcohol to your children in your home and later expect they will decline it when it is offered at a party.

• Make sure your child is aware of the legal consequences surrounding parties that allow drug and alcohol use by teens.

They should have a good understanding of the penalties associated with possession of alcohol by a minor, providing alcohol to a minor, sale of alcohol without a license (if admission is charged for entry), drunk and disorderly behavior, DUI, fighting and vandalism, etc.

- Establish a clear curfew with your child, including consequences if the curfew is broken. If your child finds he is going to miss his curfew, he should let you know, as soon as possible, where he is and when he expects to arrive. Also, if the location of the party changes, you have to be made aware of the change.

- Know how your children will get to and back from the party. It is best if they arrange to attend with at least one other friend. They should both have a pre-arranged signal to use if either of them wants to leave so they do not have to have a protracted discussion in the middle of the party.

- Be sure your children remember never to get into a car with someone who has been drinking or using drugs. This is an absolute—there is no justification that allows this rule to be broken.

- Do not allow sleepovers by your child at another child's home on the night of a party. Other parents are not necessarily on board with your policies, and sleepovers provide your child with a possible workaround to avoid your scrutiny.

• If you want to check on your children's whereabouts by phone, make sure they have to answer using a landline, not a cell phone. As an alternative, there are a number of apps you can download onto your child's Smartphone that will track his or her whereabouts. Some offer geofencing, where you can input parameters of acceptable travel and receive a text or email if he or she travels outside that area; others allow you to enter an address and receive notification alerts when your child arrives at or departs from that location. You should keep in mind that these services only indicate that your child's phone has arrived at a certain location; they do not tell you whether your child is actually with the phone. That verification will require an additional call to the phone after you receive the notification.

• Establish a code word with your child that lets him alert you to a problem without having to embarrass himself in front of a crowd. If he uses the code word, extract him from the situation in the manner you rehearsed. Do not make him explain to you why he is using the code word—there will be plenty of time for that later. Remember that in order for a code word to be effective it must be both unique enough to not crop up in everyday conversation but not so odd as to raise suspicion on the part of your child's friends when used in their presence. The example we always use for a good code word is 'sweatshirt.' He can communicate the code word to you via a phone conversation if necessary, but it is much easier and less obvious if he alerts you via a text message. In either case, when the code word is employed, you must act.

• 'No questions asked' means you do not ask questions in the heat of the moment, and that you will always do whatever it takes to keep your kids safe. It does not mean you do not have the right to discuss later what decisions went into creating the need to be rescued.

• When your children get home from socializing, you should greet them when they return. Some parents make sure their children do not have a house key when they are out at a party—they can't get back into your house unless someone opens the door for them. Even if your children were out alone, they should have to spend a few minutes with you discussing how their evening went. If you do this consistently, you will have a baseline for how your children behave after being out. Radical variations from the norm should arouse suspicion. Did something upsetting or exciting happen, or are they acting odd because they are drunk or high?

• Offer to chaperone the party. The more often your child's friends see your face at a party, the more they will see it as the norm. In our second book, *The Mother's Checklist of Drug*

Prevention, we suggest beginning this pattern when your children are young.

2.2   When Your Child Hosts A Party: Plan Ahead

• Unless the party is a surprise, your child should have an active role in the planning process. Not only does this allow a say in the activities he or she wants to include, it also offers an opportunity to discuss the responsibilities assumed when hosting a party.

• Discuss with your child what ground rules will be necessary for the party to happen. These should include start time, end time, which areas of the home will be open and which will be off-limits, how many guests he or she will invite, etc. Let your child know you expect him or her to oversee the behavior of the guests.

• Conduct a risk assessment of your home or the areas where you are going to hold the party. Areas where regular adult oversight is impossible should be closed off. If closing off areas proves difficult, arrange it so that an activity you have planned takes place there: a passageway on the side of the house could be an ideal spot for your palm reader or face painter. When assessing potential risk, try to think like a teenager. To a teen boy, a balcony is just a launch point for a leap into the pool two stories below. Balconies above pools and spas need to be closed off or closely monitored. Balconies are undesirable for another reason—the number of teen bodies that can be jammed onto one during a party can potentially be a number larger than it is able to support. Balcony collapses, while rare, are devastating and sometimes deadly. Even if there is no collapse, the news is full of stories about teen partygoers plummeting toward injury or death after falling off balconies and railings.

• Consider the use of customized wristbands for attendees. If printed beforehand and delivered to each guest as a part of the invitation, they act as a virtual guest list and ensure that only invited teens get in. There are almost limitless options available online. You may want to include on the wristband a space to write the teen's name and the phone number where you can reach his or her parents if necessary. Use a laundry pen or indelible marker to write the information on the band. This will make it easier to spot counterfeits—if the handwriting does not match, the bearer does not get in.

• You should note in your invitation that entry to the party will be a one-time event. Partygoers who choose to leave will not be allowed to re-enter. The reason for this is to limit the potential for activities you do not want going on inside the party (drinking, drug use, sex, unsupervised milling about) from taking place in another area nearby.

• When other parents call to ask questions about what kind of party you intend to have, answer their questions graciously and non-defensively. They do not think you are a bad parent; they are concerned about the safety and well-being of their children, the same way you are when you call other parents. Remember, you are on the same side. Parents who have the courage to make the call should be encouraged, not given the cold shoulder.

- Plan to provide lots of food. Unless it is a sit-down dinner party, try to choose foods that are edible without utensils or china.

- Activities and themes are a big help in minimizing the boredom and restless milling around that can result in impulsive attempts by teenage partygoers to shake things up.

- Music is not a necessity—it is a requirement. Hire a DJ or set up a playlist on your iPod. Be sure you have the technology ironed out beforehand—your iPod playlist is of no use if you cannot get it to come out of your speakers. Also, remember that while your sound system may seem adequate when you are home by yourself, the task of providing music to dozens of teens (especially at the volume they desire) may overwhelm it.

- Do not provide or allow the use of alcohol or drugs. Make sure your child is aware of the legal repercussions you face if underage alcohol use or illegal drug use occurs on your watch. There are often legal and civil penalties for adults who sponsor or allow the illegal use of alcohol on their premises.

- Familiarize yourself with your city's ordinances on parties and noise. Newport Beach, CA recently instituted a program called

LUGO—the Loud and Unruly Gatherings Ordinance—that carries stiff penalties for large gatherings that get out of control.

• Whether your security consists of a few volunteer parent chaperones or a contracted crew of trained professionals, it should be adequate and visible. Your party should not appear easy to manipulate. Lax security is one of the main reasons parties that start out as simple get-togethers end up as mini-riots when early arrivals text their friends about the lack of oversight present. Remember that party crashers will not arrive in groups of hundreds; but you can end up with hundreds of unwanted guests because of just a few social media alerts. We are not trying to suggest that every gathering of teenagers is the foreshadowing of the apocalypse, but we do want to make it clear that disasters are often the result of poor planning and oversight.

• If you do hire security, do your homework. Look for a licensed, bonded company with impeccable references. If possible, try to find one that specializes in teen parties—the more familiar they are with the challenges typically present at events of this sort, the more adept they will be at dealing with them as they arise.

• Develop an idea of how many chaperones you will need. Acceptable ratios vary, but conservative recommendations call for one chaperone for every five guests. An alternative idea is to have at least one chaperone per room. Remember that chaperones are human, and they will need to take a break occasionally—your numbers need to account for rotating assignments accordingly. If you have trouble coming up with adequate numbers of volunteer chaperones, some of our parents have had great success hiring the coaches from their child's school. This is a win-win, because the coaches are usually familiar with the attendees (good for you) and are happy to have some extra income (good for them).

• Chaperones should not drink during the event. If they consume alcohol while attempting to prevent others from doing so, it sends a mixed message. It also means they will be much less capable of doing their job.

• Have a plan for what to do if people attempt to crash your party. You and your chaperones should be willing to call 911 immediately if this happens or if events escalate beyond your ability to control them.

• Consider beforehand how you will deal with intoxicated or otherwise impaired teens. Practice what you will say to parents that you may end up having to call when you discover that their teen is not able to drive home safely. In some cases, teens can be so intoxicated that it is unsafe even to leave them unattended. The decision to call 911 if things get out of hand should be a concept you are comfortable with well before the need to do so arises. This is also the reason you want to proactively plan for adequate levels of adult oversight at your child's party—if you have done everything expected of a reasonable adult, you will have no worries about blame if the situation deteriorates and it becomes necessary to contact another parent or the police.

• Alert your local police department to the existence of the party. Many will be glad to increase patrols in your area for the duration of your event.

• Notify your neighbors about the party. Ask them to keep an eye out for any behavior they think is questionable; and to call you if they have any concerns.

• Make sure all prescription drugs in your home are under lock and key. This should be the case anyway, but especially so when guests are in your home. Even after you take the prescription drugs out of your medicine chest, you can reinforce the message that this area is off-limits by planting a marble trap inside. To build one, just put a sheet of notebook paper flat on the palm of one hand, then place about a dozen marbles in the center of the sheet and push them into your palm until the paper starts to form a basket. Gather the edges of the paper together at the top; then deftly place this fragile construction inside your medicine chest and close the door. Any guest who thinks it is a good idea to go exploring in your bathroom is going to cause a deafening cascade of marbles to bounce off the counter and floor. Even though the drugs they are looking for are not there, the marble trap still delivers the message: you are unwelcome here; stop snooping in my medicine chest. As a quieter alternative, our website's MTG Blogs page features a humorous sign to put inside your medicine cabinet to scare off snoops. You can download ours free or make one of your own—it only takes a few minutes to make it clear that this area is out of bounds.

- Move your alcohol to a safe place. Hide it, or lock it up. If your home has a bar, remove access to it completely.

2.3 When Your Child Is The Host: The Day Of The Party

• Allow invited guests only. Be aware that your child probably thinks invitations are outdated and embarrassing, but it is critical that the party not be open to all comers. That is a recipe for disaster. Do not send invitations via email or Facebook that guests can duplicate or widely forward.

• Have a guest list, check names off as they enter, and know exactly who is in your home at all times. Have at least one person checking guests in at all times and prepare for a replacement if someone needs to grab a snack or use the restroom. It only takes one minute for things to get out of control. If you are using wristbands that include handwritten information, it works best if the person who did the writing is also the person checking the bands.

• Do not allow outside beverages unless you specifically requested them. If you have solicited food and beverage contributions from guests, oversee the safety and purity of all such contributions (*i.e.*, no spiked punch, no marijuana brownies). Discourage purses, backpacks, messenger bags, etc.; or search them before allowing entry. Keep in mind that teenagers are creative when trying to sneak things into parties. One parent told us of the time she and her fellow chaperones dutifully searched each purse and backpack brought into the party, but failed to realize that the attendees had taped pints of vodka to their legs inside their pants. While it is not appropriate or possible for you to do physical pat-downs, you should not assume your job is over once your bag search is complete—regular adult oversight is still necessary throughout the evening.

• Make sure your guests realize they will not be allowed to leave the party and then return. If a guest leaves, they must be on their way. This is a good example of how wristbands can help you manage your guests—when a teen leaves, you can make the point that re-entry is not possible by removing their wristband. You may even note the time of departure on the wristband for future reference. If possible, contact the parents of guests who fail to show up, those that leave early and those that behave inappropriately (i.e. drug or alcohol use, sex, fighting, etc.).

• Circulate regularly though the party. Frequently check the out of bounds areas, including the yard and other outdoor areas. It is a good idea to monitor activity that may be going on in the cars in your parking area or on the street in front of your house.

• If someone shows up under the influence, call his or her parents, if possible. If you cannot reach their parents, call the police. You may be liable if you send them away and something happens to them.

- Do not let an intoxicated guest 'sleep it off.' Alcohol poisoning and overdose can be fatal, and laypeople cannot assess the medical condition of a teen under the influence. Call 911 for an unconscious teen—every time, all the time. You cannot let your fears of legal repercussions forestall your immediate call to 911 when necessary. You may not get a second chance to save a life.

- Occasionally, parents will use the free time they gain by dropping their kids off at your house as an opportunity to have a few cocktails at a nearby restaurant or bar. If a parent returns smelling like alcohol or obviously intoxicated, you cannot let them act as chauffeur for their child or any other. You need to keep the parent at the party for as long as possible so you can monitor their actions. Offer them some food or water or engage them in conversation for a few minutes so you can assess their condition. If you suspect that they can't drive safely, you have to talk to them gently and carefully. The last thing you want is a parent getting belligerent because they are offended, but you cannot ignore this situation. If you need backup or a second opinion, ask one of your chaperones for assistance. You might offer to have one of your chaperones drive the parent and their car home and have another follow behind to drive the first parent back when they finish. If the intoxicated parent is uncooperative and you need to call the police, please do so; but above all else, do not let any kids leave the party with that adult as their driver.

2.4 If You Are Leaving Town, But Your Child Is Not

• Make sure your child understands that you absolutely forbid parties. There should be no wiggle room on this. Be clear about the consequences for failure to live up to this expectation.

• Be very wary of allowing visitors into your home while you are away. An innocent gathering of a few friends for pizza and a movie can escalate into a Facebook and Twitter fueled debacle in minutes. Many kids never intend for this to happen, but it does with alarming frequency.

• Alert your neighbors to your absence. Ask them to keep an eye out for suspicious activity.

• Let your local police know you will be away. They will often make a point of driving by occasionally. Make sure your child knows the police will be checking. If you employ the use of a security service, let them know you will be out of town. Ask them about the possibility of increased patrols during your absence.

• Have your child stay with a friend or relative, or have a friend or relative stay in your home while you are away. At a minimum, have them check up on your children and home on a regular but random basis.

- You should already have done this, but make sure your prescription medications and alcohol are not accessible to your teen.

Part 3

What To Do When Your Kids Mess Up

3.1 Consequences

One of the most frequently asked questions at our parent presentations concerns how to go about setting up and enforcing consequences for behaviors that are unsafe or irresponsible. We understand why the question comes up so often—every kid will eventually make some bad decisions; and decisions made at parties have the capacity to be seriously irresponsible. The difficulty we have in answering these questions is that every child is unique, and so every consequence, if it is to be appropriate and effective, must be unique as well. Still, you can follow some general guidelines when you find it necessary to discipline your children.

3.2 Consequences Or Punishment?

We will use a number of terms in this discussion—consequences, penalties, punishments, etc. We will use them interchangeably, but always with the understanding that we are never referring to the act of physical punishment or emotional abuse. If you are currently hitting your children, we urge you to stop immediately and explore other ways to alter their behavior. If you insist on continuing your physical abuse of your children, we beg you to go elsewhere for your information—you will find no support here. If you ever use guilt, shame, or other emotional manipulation, please stop—it is unhealthy, unfair, and counterproductive. Your job here is to be calm and fair as you guide your children to change their behavior, not to turn them into emotionally damaged basket cases.

3.3 The Goal Of Consequences

When considering what consequences to use, the first thing to keep in mind is the end goal—of course you want to extinguish the unwanted behavior, but you ultimately want to teach your children how to manage the situation better the next time they find themselves in it. Effective punishment is not an end in itself; rather it is a consequence or experience children find unpleasant followed by education and skill building that enables them to avoid similar situations or decisions in the future.

It is physically impossible and emotionally undesirable to attempt to exert absolute control over your children's lives. It is better, when trying to change old behaviors and create new ones, to ask questions and offer occasional suggestions that your children can consider as they fulfill the debt of their consequences. The final take-away we want all kids to have when consequences conclude is that they have increased their ability to avoid negative outcomes in the future if they will only take a moment to consider their options before they act.

Obviously, this is something learned over a period of years, and older children will have far greater abilities than younger ones do. We all want our kids to be responsible, but it is unfair to hold them to a standard they are developmentally incapable of achieving. Your 13-year-old son or daughter can certainly be trusted to handle periods of unsupervised time while at home with you, but under no circumstances could they be expected to do well if left at home alone for an entire weekend.

We owe it to our children to look for situations where they can practice making decisions on their own without the potential for great harm to befall them if they get it wrong on the first try. If we start small and increase the difficulty level as they gain skills, the big decisions will come more naturally as our children grow older and their environments increase in complexity.

3.4 Consequences And Anger

It is advisable to avoid determining consequences when you are angry. The first rule of setting consequences is that you should create and discuss them with your children before you need them. We do not necessarily think you need to have pre-arranged consequences for all manners of unwanted behaviors, but for big issues like drug and alcohol use it is manageable and desirable to predetermine consequences for not following the family rules. If you regularly remind your children that there is a direct cost associated with a particular behavior, they may be less likely to act on a bad idea when it comes up.

We understand that it is a contradiction to say in one sentence that teens are almost perfectly incapable of making decisions based on future consequences of current actions (and the younger they are the less able they are to do this) and then almost immediately follow it with the suggestion that consequences can inhibit actions. We still think it worthwhile, however, to set up a structure of expectations and consequences in the hope that it may help our children make better decisions, even if it happens only occasionally.

If you try to establish consequences when you are angry or afraid, you run the risk of doing something you wish you had not when you review your actions later. Anger and rationality do not usually occur in the same instant, and your anger may drive you to create consequences that are way out of proportion to the transgression. Threatening never to let your son or daughter leave the house again may seem like a good idea when they come home at four in the morning covered in glitter and reeking of smoke, but it will lose some of its appeal in the light of day.

This is when having consequences already in place and understood by everyone will pay off—then you will not be forced into an impossible situation in the heat of the moment. Instead, you can calmly get your child into bed with the understanding, on both your parts, that discussions about decisions made and consequences resulting from those decisions can wait until morning, when cool heads and clear minds can prevail.

One other facet of consequences created in the heat of the moment we want to caution you against is the 'consequences auction'—where you sequentially bid up the severity of the consequence each time your child opens his or her mouth to protest the last penalty you put in place. What starts out as a two-week loss of privileges quickly escalates to four, six, and eight weeks each time the child being punished blurts out "That's not fair!" The problem you have is that they are right. It really is not fair to expect adolescents and teenagers, in the midst of being punished, to handle the situation with equanimity. Punishment is upsetting, and it is your job to stay calm and explain that—whether they think it is fair or not—the consequence you have outlined will be the price they pay for their behavior. If you allow your anger to get the better of you when your child calls you unfair, you run the risk of reacting inappropriately and becoming less effective as a parent. We are not saying that disrespect should be the order of the day in your home, but we urge you to cut your children a little slack over what they say when they receive a punishment.

3.5 If You Say You're Going To Do It, Do It

Perhaps the most critical aspect of setting effective consequences is to enforce them once you put them in place. Literally days before we wrote this sentence, the son of a friend, during a discussion about consequences, said of his parents, "It doesn't really matter what they say. I know they'll never do it." It is a worthwhile exercise in any discussion about punishment to take a moment to reflect on your current record of accomplishment. Do you really follow through after you lay out a consequence, or do you fold as soon as it becomes uncomfortable or inconvenient to enforce?

We think it is appropriate to say that if you do not intend to enforce the consequence in the first place, don't waste everyone's time acting as if you will. Failing to enforce consequences may even be worse than doing nothing at all. If you institute consequences and then do not enforce them, it shows that you knew the right thing to do but were just too lazy or unconcerned to follow through. Remember always that your actions speak louder than your words, and if you talk a good game but play a poor one, you run the risk of indicating to your children that they really are not important enough to deserve your very best efforts.

It can be equally challenging when parents attempt to institute consequences only to discover that their child refuses to submit to them. It can get very tense when confrontations of this type arise, but it is imperative that parents not lose control of the situation. If you find yourself trying to enforce consequences with an oppositional teen, you may have to bring in outside help. A therapist or counselor can help you find ways to maintain your authority; but the severest cases might force you to involve the aid of the police to maintain order. If your child is violent or insists on roaming at will, this may be your only option to keep him or her safe.

The most important point here is not to let the child be the most powerful party. Teens are incapable of managing situations of this complexity and are unable to imagine how such behaviors will affect their current development and potential to live as skilled adults. That is the job of the parent, and this is a job where we cannot fail.

3.6   Keep The Children And Their Behaviors Separate

One point that can get lost in the storm of bad behavior and the following consequences is that the behaviors and the children are two different things. It can be easy when punishing children to leave them with the impression that they, rather than the behavior they exhibited, are undesirable or unwanted. It may sound like New Age blather, but we always want our children to understand that the whole reason we go through so much upset when they do something wrong is because we love them and want the best for them. Small mistakes in judgment, left unaddressed, can become the stuff of terribly destructive habits later.

It is important that we never label our children with their behaviors—stupid behaviors do not indicate that children are stupid, and we should not indicate that this is what we believe. Everyone does ill-considered things from time to time, and we would do well as parents to think back to the last time we did something ridiculously dumb before we apply inappropriate labels to our children when they stray from responsible decisions and actions.

3.7 Consequences Also Impact You

We encourage parents to remember that it will not just be your children paying a consequence here—you are the ones who will have to monitor the enforcement and intercede when conditions are not met. If your older children drive to school each day, taking away their driving privileges means you are now on the hook for getting them there. You may be tempted to set it up so that you only allow them to drive to school and back, but you now face the ongoing task of monitoring whether they are following your conditions. The temptation for your teens to stray will be constant, and you may just be setting up a situation where you will now have to punish a new violation when your children ignore a previous consequence. The point is that it can be difficult to set up consequences that do not extract more costs from you than they do from your children.

3.8 Treat Consequences Like Goals

When you do finally choose a consequence, either from the list we provide in this section or one you create, be sure that it meets some basic parameters. We think you should treat consequences just like goals—they should be written down and clearly defined; the reason for their necessity should be clear; they should have a time limit; they should be proportional and achievable; you should celebrate their completion; and new expectations should be discussed as the process concludes.

3.9 Write It Down

By writing everything down, you eliminate the confusion that can crop up later about what is actually required in order to satisfy the consequence. The last argument you want to find yourself in is whether you took the car away for one week or two; and heaven forbid you get it wrong. It is highly likely your children have already deemed your actions to be unfair, and changing the rules in midstream will cement in their minds the notion that they are right. Many parents also suggest that you have your children sign the outline of consequences—that way, you eliminate the chance that they will claim they misunderstood what you meant later on.

3.10 Restate Why Consequences Are Necessary

As you outline the consequences you are instituting, take the time to reiterate why they are necessary in the first place. If your expectations and rules are clearly stated, it will also be clear when your children violate them. In each instance, you should go over where your expectations were not met and which rules were broken. You want it to be clear that you are not punishing them because it is fun for you; you are doing it because the behaviors in question are so dangerous, unhealthy, disrespectful or inappropriate that to let them pass without penalty would cause your children harm, immediately or in the future. Let them know that you are sad that their behavior requires that consequences be present in their lives, but also be very clear that it is the result of a choice they made—this is their weight to carry.

A big problem teens tell us they have with their parents' rules, expectations, and consequences is that they do not understand why it has to be that way—it often seems that their parents are just making it up as they go. If you take the time to explain the reasoning behind a family rule or parental expectation, it will reduce the amount of rebellion that rule elicits.

An example we regularly use in our parent presentations concerns curfews. If you tell a senior in high school that his or her curfew is midnight, you can expect them to challenge it as too early. You can make your point in one of two ways. First, you can tell your teen that the curfew is midnight because you say it is—there is no room for discussion. On the other hand, you can explain that your curfew is midnight because statistics show that teenagers die behind the wheel at a much higher rate after midnight than before, and for that reason, you want your child home before his or her risk of dying skyrockets. Which reason do you think will elicit less rebellion—the mandate of a fixed, unexplained time; or the explanation of how concerned you are about your child's safety?

3.11 Set A Time Limit

The punishment should have a defined beginning and end. When you place a time limit on the consequence, you give your children a clear finish line. Open-ended punishments are really just psychological torture—people can grow desperate in situations where they never know when or if something unpleasant will end. Remember that the goal here is to change behaviors, but how can your children ever show you they have learned a lesson from their punishment if the punishment never ends?

One mother we spoke with was in the ninth month of punishing her daughter for using alcohol at a party in her junior year, and the mom admitted she had no clear end in sight. She was terrified that if she let her daughter go out with her friends again she would run the risk of her daughter drinking again. Her feeling was that if it happened once, it could happen again. It might be true that if she never let her daughter go out with her friends again, she could avoid a repeat of the behavior, but the cost of that success would be enormous.

Adolescents change so rapidly and extremely that if you are still punishing a teenager for something she did nine months ago, you probably are not even punishing the same child that committed the infraction! Consequences that stretch out forever communicate to your children that you have lost confidence in their ability to make good choices—ever. The penalty should be unpleasant, certainly, but it must eventually end so they can have the opportunity to grow from the experience.

3.12 Consequences Must Be Proportional

The magnitude of the consequence should be directly proportional to the behavior that brought about the need for it to be enforced. In order to remain valid as a parent you have to be seen by your children, at a minimum, as marginally reasonable. If you institute massive consequences for minimally offensive behavior, your children will come to view you as unreasonable at best and insane at worst. In addition, if you fire your best shot in the beginning, what options do you have left if the problem escalates? Keep in mind that teaching your children how to live within the confines of your rules and expectations is a process of developing skills, and that usually does not happen in one fell swoop.

This is an area where it is particularly difficult to give advice about what is right and what is wrong—every parent has a different opinion about what is appropriate and proportional in a given instance. The best we can advise here is to compare notes with other parents when trying to determine what level of intensity is appropriate when applying a consequence for a particular behavior, but you should be cautious about who you choose to confide in. Some parents might be quick to identify your teen as 'the kid with the drinking problem' if you go out shopping for advice the first time you find out he or she attended a party where alcohol was present. You can find reams of information about consequences online, but try to stick to rational, nationally recognized sites if you choose that route.

If after comparison you find that you fall seriously short or radically overshoot, you may want to consider amending your views when it comes to putting consequences in place. One rule of thumb to keep in mind is that the consequence should not last longer than your children's capacity to remember the reason you are punishing them. A five-year-old child will not be able to relate a current consequence to something he or she did a week ago; a fifteen-year-old child certainly can. If your teenager misses a curfew, setting an earlier curfew for the next two weeks seems reasonable, and it has the benefit of pertaining directly to the behavior in question as well. Your teen should also understand that further failures in this area would lead to increasingly intense consequences.

3.13 When Consequences End, Celebrate!

When the consequence concludes, you should celebrate its end. We know it may seem odd to use the word celebrate in reference to a punishment, but that is exactly how we think you should handle it. By celebrating the end of a consequence, you communicate to your children that while the punishment itself may have been unpleasant, its end represents a new beginning, a new opportunity for them to prove they have the ability to handle the same situation more effectively when confronted with it in future.

This is actually an exercise in forgiveness. Once you address an unwanted behavior and its cost is paid, it is time to move on and provide new opportunities for your children to show off their new abilities. This does not mean a return to the status quo, however. As a part of teaching your children how to make new choices, you should discuss with them your continued expectations concerning their behavior and reiterate that your family rules are still in place.

You may also have to discuss what you will be doing to ensure their success in the future. These discussions should pertain directly to what circumstances you imagine led to past difficulties and what you can both do in the future to prevent their recurrence. For example: if your child was drinking alcohol at an unsupervised party, you will want to institute a policy that requires you to verify that adequate, appropriate supervision is in place at future parties that child wants to attend.

This will usually lead to discussions about you not trusting your children, and it is important not to be trapped in this box canyon of an argument. The common lament of most teens caught in this situation is, "How can I prove I'm trustworthy if you never trust me?" The reality, however, is that this is not really a matter of whether you trust them or not, it is the situation itself that is giving you pause. Point out to your teens that your concern is not with them as individuals—you do not think any teen would do well in an unsupervised party environment, and it is your job to make sure your children do not find themselves facing that challenge. Parties where teenagers use alcohol and drugs are unsafe and unhealthy by definition and concerned parents do not allow their children to spend time in that kind of environment. Trust is not the issue here; the safety and health of your children is the issue, and in that area, you hold the trump cards.

3.14 Choosing A Consequence

Now that we have covered the basic parameters of effective consequences, we need to discuss how to go about choosing a consequence. We've compiled a list of the most frequently suggested ideas that we've gathered from both parents and teens on what should be considered when it comes to helping children realize the cost of bad decisions. Again, keep in mind this is a general list—what one child sees as torture might go unnoticed by another. We have also divided the list into two parts: things to take away and tasks to accomplish.

3.15   Things To Take Away

• Anything that starts with a lower case i—iPad, iPhone, iPod, iPod Touch, etc.

• Any other communication devices, especially cell phones and Smartphones. This can include, in extreme cases, closing the account entirely.

• Any other music technology, MP3 players, etc.

• Anything related to transportation, including bikes, cars, driver's licenses, etc.

• Computer time that is not school related. This is hard to control if your children's computers are in their rooms and not in a communal area of the home. Locate computers where you can monitor them. Texting and Instant Messaging should be limited to school related issues or eliminated entirely.

• Any sports equipment, including but not limited to surfboards, skateboards, bikes, tennis racquets, golf clubs, etc.

• Musical instruments.

- Video games. Not just Xbox, PlayStation, or Wii systems, but also hand-held devices. Remember that many video games are now played on phones, so you may have to take away the phone or insist on the deletion or game apps if you choose this as a consequence.

- Participation in team sports. We think you should consult the coach of the team for his/her input—together you may be able to come up with a consequence that is unpleasant for your child but doesn't hurt the team. Again, be careful about how much information you share with the coach. Less is more here, for the most part. If the team or its members are part of the problem, however, the activity may have to cease entirely.

- Contact with friends outside school hours.

- Any upcoming social event, including prom, winter formals, games, plays, etc.

- Plans for vacations or camps.

- Classes outside of school that the child values, such as dance, tennis, theater, etc.

- Family events that the child values, including visits from or to extended family.

- Travel, including school trips.

- Access to a particular type of clothing. If being fashionable is high on your child's list of passions, a trip to a local low-end department store for a few new school outfits might be the worst punishment you could devise.

- Any allowance or monetary support you may have been providing.

- Curfew time: arriving home late one evening means earlier curfews the next few times.

- Purchases your children may have planned—you can cancel or delay these.

- Anything else your particular child has a deep interest in or passion for.

3.16 Remember Your Purpose

Taking things away from children as a means of punishing them seems to be the default position for most of the parents we talk to, and we certainly feel it has a place in your menu of responses to unwanted behavior. We also feel, however, that simply taking things away does little to teach them new behaviors. When you take something away, take the time to establish the behaviors your children must exhibit in order to win back the possession or activity they have lost. This allows them to practice the behavior you are trying to instill in them, and it gives them and you a way to gauge how well they have understood what you want from them. Remember, this is not just your children serving their time—it is about building skills.

We think the second punishment option—tasks to accomplish—can potentially do a much better job of teaching your children the error of their ways while also teaching them something new about their behaviors—both the ones that preceded the consequence and those you hope will follow it. While it is important to make every attempt to have the consequence pertain directly to the behavior in question, that will not always be possible. Some items mentioned here would be effective simply because your children find them unpleasant, and that is the lesson—bad decisions lead to unpleasant consequences. Make sure to discuss with your children the notion that they can avoid further unpleasantness by making better decisions.

3.17   Tasks To Accomplish

• Have your child research a topic that pertains to the offense he or she committed and then write an essay on that topic. For example, if your son was caught riding in a car with an impaired teen at the wheel, have him research and write about the societal costs associated with drunk driving. Keep in mind that if you assign a writing project, you do not just want your teen to cut and paste a bunch of information from the Internet and call it an essay. This writing should be a result of their research and be written in their own words. This will obviously mean more work for you!

• Have your child see or listen to someone speak about a subject that pertains to the behavior in question and write about what he or she learned. If your daughter drove after drinking, you could have her attend an event sponsored by Mothers Against Drunk Driving. Following this, have her write about what it would be like to cause the death of another child while driving drunk. Have her specifically address what she would say to the mother of that child and how she would explain her actions. Alternatively, you could have her imagine she has killed a husband and father while driving drunk and have her write about how it would feel to explain to that man's children why daddy will not be coming home any more.

- Have your child do volunteer work in an area associated with his or her behavior. A night spent handing out pamphlets at a DUI checkpoint can be a powerful reminder of what consequences can result from irresponsible choices—especially those involving alcohol and cars.

- Volunteer work of any type can be a way to help your teenager reflect on the consequences of his or her behavior. A few ideas you might consider are visiting with the elderly, reading to sick adults or children, tutoring a student struggling in an area in which your child excels, or helping out at a local veteran's organization. Keep in mind that the last thing any of these people need is a sulking teenager who is making everyone's day harder. If your teen cannot handle this task maturely, please skip it and choose another that inflicts less damage on the unsuspecting recipients.

- Have your children do tasks around the house in order to pay off their punishment debt. These can be anything you need done, but the more onerous the better. The tasks chosen should be over and above the normal chores you expect them to perform. If you choose this as an option, do not ignore the opportunity it presents to offer praise after they finish the task. Remember, children thrive when you compliment them.

3.18 Thoughts On Consequences

These ideas are just a starting point. You know your children better than you know anyone else, and that means you possess great insight into what will have the most profound impact on them. We think the most effective consequences will be a combination of the two types. First, you take something away. Then, they must prove they deserve to have the missing item or privilege returned by completing a task or fulfilling an obligation you lay out. This is also the perfect time to set new goals and discuss new expectations about future behavior.

Always strive to keep in mind what your role in this whole process is—you are the calm, mature guide leading your children to new and better decision-making. You want to remind your children that all this turmoil resulted from a decision they made, and you want to make it clear that you fully expect they will do better next time. In this way, poor decisions made by your children become opportunities for your relationship to grow stronger.

Part 4

Peer Pressure

4.1 Peer Pressure: The World's Most Misunderstood Term

As we attempt to develop and strengthen our relationships with our children, one of the more challenging issues we must understand is the pressure they face when in the presence of their friends and classmates.

Peer pressure is a concept that parents often misunderstand. It is tempting to approach the issue by interpreting the words literally: peer pressure is influence exerted upon your child by another child of approximately the same age and situation. Peer pressure is cited as the reason for almost everything we fear or do not like in our children. We blame it for causing drug and alcohol use, premature sexual activity, cheating, theft, violence, and rebellion.

Our goal is not to try to convince you that peer pressure is not a powerful force in your child's life—it is. What we want to do is redefine the nature of peer pressure and give you ways to minimize its impact. It is a mistake to think that your child's peers are constantly trying to get him or her to do a particular thing or think a specific way. While this certainly happens, it is not the primary driving force. Peer pressure is less about pressure applied directly by peers and more about pressure felt by your child around issues that involve his or her peers. In other words, it is not so much what our child's peers think, it is what he or she thinks they think. The source of most peer pressure does not come from the outside; it originates in your child's imagination.

We must constantly keep in mind that what our children seek above all else is acceptance by their peers. Humans have a biological drive to join the group, and we constantly assess situations with an eye toward what will make us more acceptable to the group we want to join. The big confusion that surrounds the issue of peer pressure is the assumption that the group is clear in its demands—it almost never is. It is more likely that the sole option apparent to the child is to imagine what type of behavior will win the favor or attention of the group and then test it to see how it works. Unfortunately, if the group is engaged in unsafe, unhealthy behaviors (like drinking and using drugs at a party) those are the first behaviors that a child trying to join the group will test for effectiveness.

However, there are two reasons why it is important not to view your children as the innocent victims of a negative campaign of influence emanating from their friends and classmates. First, it is certainly not helpful to view teens as hapless victims suffering the whims of their peers. Second, it appears that the opposite is often the case. Evidence exists that says children do not necessarily experience peer pressure that comes as a surprise after they align themselves with a particular group; rather they will survey the landscape and choose a group of peers that is already doing what they wanted to do in the first place. Once they have identified the group they want to join, it is at that point they will start to mimic the actions of that particular group in an effort to gain acceptance.

As you read this section, we want you to keep this redefinition of peer pressure in mind. It might help to think about peer pressure within the context of the larger term *social pressure*; and since our kids are most social with their peers, social pressure for them is usually peer oriented. We think this will help you understand the challenges your children face as they navigate their teen years; and that it will make you better able to help them face those challenges effectively. When you have a clear idea of how the problem presents itself, you can more accurately influence your teens' decision-making process for the good. If you waste all of your time and credibility inaccurately blaming your child's peers for their influence, you will miss the opportunity to help him or her understand the complex dance of fitting in without sacrificing the person he or she is in order to do so.

4.2　What Areas Does Peer Pressure Affect?

Peer pressure is not a single issue—it can exist within an almost limitless number of contexts: drugs and alcohol, sex, academic effort, cheating, race, athletics, fashion, music, cars, hairstyles, honesty, religion, politics, family issues, employment, materialism, and so on. The things we need to keep in mind are that our children are constantly feeling the pressure to fit in and that these pressures come at them from a thousand different directions.

To know your son, you need to know his peers and observe how he acts when he is with them. What group does he migrate toward when he arrives at school? Does his demeanor change the minute he is in the presence of his friends? Realize that if his behavior changes, he is often not consciously aware of it—he is just doing whatever he perceives as necessary to mesh with the crowd; to become acceptable by becoming alike.

Remember that you cannot always trust what your son or daughter tells you about the amount and variety of social pressure he or she may be experiencing. One thing teens do not want to feel or admit is a sense of being under someone or something else's control. Many of our students insist they feel no pressure to conform to a standard of dress while simultaneously wearing clothes that could essentially act as a mirror for the child standing next to them.

A few years ago, we visited a school where all the boys wore a very particular style of ball cap, but not just any cap would do. The fabric had to be perfectly aged and faded, the logo had to be acceptably cool, and the bill had to be frayed along the edge to a very specific degree. When asked about the hats' significance, the students were studies in innocence: "They don't mean anything—they're just hats." Sure they are!

We witnessed a much more powerful example of peer conformity at another school about ten years ago. The power of the example stemmed from the fact that the behavior exhibited was so distinctly strange that no group would do it spontaneously; so, any student who chose to participate did so in an effort to gain acceptance and status.

The behavior consisted of each student rubbing a pencil eraser on the top of his or her desk in order to create a pile of eraser crumbs. When an adequate amount had accumulated, the student would gather them up and deposit them in an Altoids tin. This is not a joke—the majority of this class was totally absorbed in this activity. The more passionate participants had graduated from regular sized Altoids tins to the extra-large industrial size. In order to be sure none of their precious crumbs were lost, they all employed multiple rubber bands to keep their tins securely closed. The students with the most eraser crumbs gained status from their success.

It's hard to imagine how this weird behavior got started, and you might be tempted to write it off as the result of little kids learning how to write and erase, but there's one problem with that theory—these were seventh and eighth graders. Some of the students engrossed in this erasing ritual were just one year away from high school, where such behavior would mark them as deranged freaks; but in this one environment, it marked them as successful and accepted.

This example highlights so many important points about peer pressure, but the most powerful one is this: any behavior the group deems to be important (no matter how odd) will become the standard by which acceptance is measured.

What every adult needs to remember is that the pressure to join is so powerful, so overriding, that little thought is given to the rightness or wrongness of the behavior required for membership—it can stretch from positive behaviors like high academic performance to destructive behaviors like drug and alcohol use.

We need to be careful not to dismiss something as unimportant simply because it seems trivial to us. The measure of the value of an activity or behavior is the gravity our children assign to it; and acceptance by the group is of the utmost importance.

4.3   Teen Parties: Peer Pressure At Its Very Best

Because of the nature of our jobs as drug educators, one of the more pervasive forms of social pressure we see teens struggle with is the party scene. Teens can gain huge social capital just by being present at a party, and their stock soars if they are the host or the person who provided part or all of the drugs and alcohol. Unfortunately, teens who host parties rarely imagine things could get out of control—and yet they often do. The results can be tragic: shootings, stabbings, fights, drug overdoses, alcohol overdoses, massive property damage, sexual activity, and sexual assaults regularly occur at these unsupervised parties.

As parents, it can be hard for us to imagine why our children would even want to attend parties where such awful outcomes can occur, but it is our job to understand what it is our teens are seeking when they attend a party. Again, there is not just one dynamic at play here. Parties represent social acceptance, or at least a few points on the social scorecard. Parties that feature drugs and alcohol represent adult behavior, and despite their regular protestations, teens constantly seek to appear grown up. Add to this the fact that parties are commonly seen as payback for the huge academic effort the attendees have put in during the school week. They often learn this directly from their parents—"I've worked hard, and damn it, I'm going to let it rip!" Parents often do not realize how closely their kids are watching them. Many adults can remember sitting on the stairs as young children, watching through the balusters while their parents and their friends socialized at parties. Alcohol often flowed freely, and the message could not have been clearer: this is how adults have fun and unwind from a hard week at work.

Today, teen parties have taken on a life of their own. Teens no longer need to look only to their parents for cues on how to socialize; the teen party has achieved legacy status. Teens also no longer view parties as a privilege; they see them as a right. Parents we have seen who offer a quid pro quo—if you do well in school, we'll look the other way when you drink or do drugs at weekend parties—reinforce this impression. The sad fact is that these parents are ignoring the biggest threat posed by teen use—the unknown damage that will only be realized years or decades later.

We cannot expect this situation to change if we just sit and wait. If we want to alter the dynamic of teen parties, we need to get better at managing the expectations and behaviors of our children. If we are to lessen the potential for parties to hurt our children, we must strengthen our resolve and hone our skills at managing how and with whom our teens party.

4.4 Parties Are Not Evil—But They Can Be Dangerous

The main goal here is not to keep your children from socializing at major events like parties, rather it is to allow them the opportunity to experience different kinds of temptations and decision making while at the same time keeping them away from drug and alcohol use, inappropriate sexual activity, and violence. This is an incredibly difficult balancing act—you need to create an atmosphere of controlled freedom.

Your children will learn the skills necessary to manage their social lives only if you give them the chance to make decisions and relish the rewards of correct choices or suffer the consequences of incorrect ones. The hardest aspect of this process for parents to deal with is that teens can only make real decisions outside your direct oversight; yet sometimes when they are out of your direct oversight they can make choices that have the potential to end or severely damage their lives.

Parties are not by definition evil. In fact, they represent one of the more enticing opportunities children have during their teen years. Because they are open-ended and somewhat unpredictable, they have a mystery and possibility about them that is exciting. They hold the potential for romance, risk, new friends, and social connection—all the elements teens find so attractive. They are new, they are social, and they are adult. In essence, they are perfect. Yet what teens see as perfect can leave their parents paralyzed with fear.

As we said, some of the choices present at parties are simply dangerous, and drug and alcohol use are right at the top of our list of threats. While your children may not use drugs or drink alcohol, they surely know or are aware of kids who do. Do not ignore the complexities of their world just because they are not overtly displaying the behaviors associated with direct participation. If you assume or act like the problem does not exist simply because it is not currently affecting your children directly, you deprive yourself of the opportunity to discuss the issue with them.

Teens find risk and danger attractive, yet they lack the experience and the demeanor to choose wisely in the face of temptation. As parents, we need to find ways to allow our children the freedom to make decisions in areas where they have little or no experience so they can learn the process of weighing options and choosing an appropriate path. This process has to start small and increase in complexity as you see your children gain skill.

Of course, your children are going to try to convince you that the only way they will be able to attend a party without dying of embarrassment is for you to stay as far away as possible for as long as possible—permanently, if that can be arranged. They are convinced they can handle the decisions required without any help. You, on the other hand, want to be attached to them at the hip for the duration of the event. Neither option will work—you have to find a way to balance both your needs in the best way possible.

The guidelines we propose in this book are probably not going to please your teen. He or she will typically see them as draconian and controlling. Your job is to convey the message (as kindly as is possible) that if your child wants to attend parties, he or she will need to do so in a way that keeps you sane. The suggestions outlined in this book are a way to maintain your emotional well-being while not destroying your teen's ability to socialize.

4.5 To Battle Peer Pressure, You've Got To Have Your Child's Back

Although teens sometimes make it seem that their parents do not matter and their friends do, the most commonly cited role models teens look to for guidance are their parents. How you conduct yourself, how you measure success, and how you determine right and wrong play a big part in how your children act, how they view themselves, and how they respond to pressure from their peers.

As we wrote this book there was a story playing out online about a father in Germany who chose to support his son in a unique way—he dressed up in a skirt and went for a walk. It seems the five-year-old son had always liked wearing dresses, and felt perfectly OK doing so until the family moved from Berlin to a small town in the countryside. The people in the small town were less open to the idea of a young boy wearing girls' clothes, and the son became the object of ridicule and bullying.

Worried about the toll the bullying was taking on his son, the dad did the only thing he thought would have an impact—he put on a skirt and took his son out for a walk through town.

Following the release of this story, there were many questions asked: Should little boys wear girls' clothes? Should the dad be supporting this behavior? Should he be ashamed because his son is different?

The bottom line, to us, is that none of this matters—not even a little bit. Given the choice between wearing boys' clothes or girls' clothes, the son chose dresses. He may grow out of this; he may not. The point is, the father realized that what his son really needed was not fashion tips, nor did he need the one man in the world he looked up to above all others showing shame over his behavior. What he needed was protection and support, and that is what his dad gave him.

You may not think Gawker was correct in choosing this man as their 'Father of the Year', but it is hard to dispute that he did something that required courage; and his actions showed his son that his dad's love for him knows no social boundaries and will not yield to the assaults of bullies. We like this story because it shows a parent taking an action that in many circles would be unpopular, but he did it anyway. Doing the right thing when the right thing is blatantly obvious does not require as much character as does doing the right thing when the situation is complicated, confusing, and riddled with social pressure.

How we act in the face of pressure from our peers does a lot more to teach our kids how to deal with social pressure from their peers than any lecture we give ever will. Whatever happens in the future, this little boy will be sure of one thing: his dad is his biggest fan and his bravest advocate, and when tested, he showed courage and protected him. Everybody wants someone to have his or her back. If kids can have the confidence their parents are doing the job, they will not need to look elsewhere as they get older for someone who will. What a great dad to have as a role model—everyone should be so lucky.

4.6 Mixed Messages—Your Kids Are Watching You

If we want to maintain our relationships with our children and continue to influence their decisions, we have to remain valid and trustworthy. One of the best ways to lessen the impact of peer pressure is to avoid mixed messages. We cannot act one way and expect that our children will act another. If we present ourselves in a way that is disingenuous, we may cause our children to seek honesty elsewhere. Since adolescent relationships often do not operate on a level of deep emotional openness, they may think that the relationships they have with their peers are more honest than the ones they have with us are.

How we act often becomes the measure of who we are. We cannot falsely claim illness in order to get out of an undesirable obligation and then expect our children always to tell the truth. We cannot get plastered at a party and then expect our children to listen to our lectures on the dangers of alcohol abuse. We cannot cheat on our taxes and then expect our children to resist the temptation to get something they want without earning it.

Our children constantly look to us for guidance, but they rarely do so by directly asking for our advice. While they may occasionally come to us seeking input on how to handle things, they are more likely to watch us on a daily basis for clues about how we actually get things done. What we show them as we go about living our lives will teach them the lessons of what we believe much more powerfully than what we tell them ever will.

The last thing we want to do in our efforts to lessen the influence of their peers is give them evidence that we are less trustworthy than their peers are.

4.7 There Is A Competition Here—You Vs. Your Child's Peers

Your teens typically cannot be true to you and true to their friends at the same time. This means they have to choose between two competing desires. Neither desire is necessarily wrong—they are just in conflict. Your relationship with your children will play a big part in how much influence you have over the decisions they make, but you should remember that you will have a hard time competing with their friends, especially in circumstances when they are alone with their friends and there is no adult oversight present.

Our children will sometimes go to great lengths to avoid the appearance of being different; to avoid any sign of uniqueness or vulnerability. This is the birth of the affected state of coolness exhibited by so many kids, but their mask of coolness is really a mask of fear. They dare not exhibit behaviors that will cause them to become the target of derision, so they stop taking risks and behaving in any way that appears eccentric. In many cases, this means an abandonment of the old self. The quirky kid you used to adore can become the insufferable clone of his friends in a very short time.

This does not mean one decision or action should define your child in your eyes—he will constantly switch back and forth in his loyalties. He can easily see the same situation two completely different ways depending upon what group he is with at the time. We want to teach our children the lessons they need to survive in the end; they want to survive their culture. We want them to value hard work; they want to listen to the right music. We want them to be true to themselves; they want to wear the right clothes or have the right Smartphone. What we value and what our children and their peer group value are rarely the same things.

These conflicting tensions are constantly pulling your child in one direction or another, and trying to balance all the warring influences can be exhausting for him. The experience can be emotionally wrenching as well. Most parents and children are extremely close when the children are young. As they grow older, though, the children will sometimes find the pull of the group irresistible; and they often cannot gain the favor of the group and stay close to their parents at the same time.

Unfortunately, this happens right when it would be most helpful to keep that relationship going; and this disconnect from parents takes an emotional toll on teens, even when they are unable to understand or even acknowledge the existence of this conflict. The critical thing for you to remember is that you cannot invest any time into the idea that your children do not need you just because the say so, or because they act in such a way as to indicate that you are an insult to their very existence. If your children tell you that they hate you—or that every word out of your mouth makes them want to die of embarrassment—you need to don the parental body armor. When you believe what your kids say in this area, you abandon them to their peers.

The other most critical thing to remember when kids say horrible things to us is never to succumb to the temptation to respond in kind. If we lash out emotionally at our kids, we can do some serious damage. One of the things about being a parent is that we know our kids so well we have the insight required to cause great harm if the goal is to wound them back after they wound us. This may be one of our biggest and hardest to resist errors. When our kids say hurtful things to us, they are testing our commitment to the relationship. If we respond in kind, we fail the test.

4.8 Peer Pressure Works Both Ways

One aspect of peer pressure parents fear most is its almost universal ability to influence how their kids act as members of a group, but that universality also means the powerful influences our kids' peers have can work for the good as effectively as they can the bad. One of the greatest features of our jobs as drug educators is that our travels expose us to some of the best academic students in the country. The schools we work with offer stellar faculties, fabulous campuses, outstanding technical resources and are blessed with the freedom to admit students who have shown a past ability and continued desire to succeed academically.

Because of this, the academic climate at these schools is almost exclusively one of success; and this is not just the expectation of the faculties and the parents, it is also that of the students. This leads to a lot of peer pressure to succeed academically, and we are not referring to the high stress, gut-wrenching fear of failure some people suffer under the weight of such expectations. These are students with an established record of accomplishment and success, and most of them thrive in this climate. If circumstances arise where a student struggles academically, resources are available to put that student back on a path to success. However, any student who decides academic achievement no longer matters will almost immediately feel stress because of this failure to adhere to the norms of academic success observed by his or her peers.

We rush to point out that we are not trying to be disingenuous or act like everything is perfect in these schools. All schools face difficulties, and the ones we work with are not exceptions. In a 2011 blog, Pat Bassett, the head of the National Association of Independent Schools, observed that, "The problem of adolescent drinking has been endemic in independent schools forever, a learned behavior from their parents, the social elite, and their Dionysian older siblings — and a problem pretty much ignored until some infraction (*e.g.*, drinking at the prom) causes a disciplinary crisis."

The fact that alcohol use is endemic at many high-end private schools is not lost on us—we wrote this book specifically to address that very point; but we have to remember to take the good with the bad. Yes, there are substance abuse issues in almost all schools, but the schools we work with still have an impressive number of academically driven and successful students, and those students inspire a positive form of peer pressure.

Unfortunately, the same cannot be said for a heartbreaking number of other schools we regularly see and hear about in southern California and across the country. Many communities battle a different kind of peer pressure; one that does not value academic excellence. In fact, members of some communities see academic success as a stigma, a reason for students to be ridiculed and browbeaten. In situations like these, it is a lot harder to convince a teen that academic effort will pay off in the end.

Unfortunately for the parents of these kids, the long run is not a strong suit for teenagers—most are hopelessly mired in the present; and if the present says that you will be stigmatized for trying hard in school, it takes a really strong teen with a deeply realized sense of self to stand up to that kind of pressure. The overwhelming majority of teens are terrified to stand out as different; to be at odds with what their culture says is cool. Parents of these children face the daunting challenge of helping their kids find a peer group that values school and the attendant effort required to succeed there.

While this may be difficult to do, the alternative is bleak. For a teen without a high school diploma, future prospects are exceedingly dim.

This doesn't mean all is lost, it just means a lot more work for parents who find themselves facing these challenges. Positive, dedicated mentors and role models are present in any community, and hardworking peers who struggle to succeed exist no matter where you go. The hard part is locating them and convincing your child to take advantage of them. The payoff comes when parents can get their children aligned with a group of other like-minded teens working to succeed—these groups have the power to show your child that they are not crazy to try and that failure is not a foregone conclusion. It takes strong, dedicated parents and kids to do this kind of work, but the rewards of exposing your child to positive peer influence is without equal.

The same is true for any group of young people that shows a positive influence over your child. Our daughter is utterly in love with theater—the music, the stories, the costumes, the backstage crafts, the actors—you name it. If it has anything to do with theater, she thinks it is magical. Our experience over the past few years has been that the kids she meets when she is involved with putting on a play are generally kind, talented, hardworking and above all, positively influential peers. Almost every one of them does well in school, and the parents of most of these kids are committed to the idea that if their children want to continue to have the freedom to participate in the productions they must maintain their grades in school and stay out of trouble the rest of the time. In our opinion, that is a decidedly outstanding peer group.

The other great thing about theater is that in order to get up on a stage and deliver lines effectively, actors have to take risks; they have to put themselves out there in a vulnerable, emotional, thrilling way. For most of the kids we've talked to, it's a rush for them to do so; and it's our opinion that if a boy or a girl can get a dopamine and adrenaline surge from being on stage, they're less likely to feel the need to get it by abusing drugs and alcohol.

Peers can have positive effects on our children in other, less direct ways as well. One of the most powerful protective factors a teen can have when she finds herself in a difficult social situation is the presence of at least one other like-minded friend. This friend does not have to speak out in defense of your daughter; in fact, she does not have to speak at all. Your daughter, simply by knowing the other supportive friend is in the room, will draw strength from that friend's presence. Really, this is nothing more than the magic of knowing she is not alone.

Other examples of positive peer pressure abound, and many of them revolve around sports. While professional and college sports are riddled with stories of drug and alcohol use, and while the athletes who play these sports sometimes seem to suffer a complete lack of maturity and life skills, there are numerous other stories about how athletes use their sport as a way to stay sober, motivated, in school, goal-oriented, and team-centered.

This discussion of positive peer pressure highlights how hard it is for both children and their parents to get a handle on the complexities of social pressure. It can be difficult to see, at first, that the kids with so much positive academic influence over your child at school are the same ones that can exert negative influence at a party on Saturday night. As we said earlier, this is why we cannot resort to the simplistic exercise of labeling a child as a particular type of person due to one action he or she took. Your child does not go to school with a bunch of bad kids; he or she goes to school with a bunch of good kids who have the capacity to make spectacularly bad decisions when left unsupervised at a party.

We must also realize that our children can find this conflict confusing as well. At school, they can watch all week as a fellow student does everything right—he works hard, gets good grades, and has great relationships with faculty members and administrators; yet on the weekend at a party they might witness that same student drinking or using drugs. It can be easy for our children to transfer their views of that student's actions during the week to his actions on the weekend—he does everything else right, so this must be right as well.

The upshot is this: the quality of peer influence is much less about the nature of the children than it is about the nature of the situation. Good kids, when confronted with certain temptations, can make bad decisions. It falls to us to be sure that the environments our children experience are beneficial to them. We can affect the decisions our children make by increasing opportunities to spend time in positive situations and minimizing opportunities to spend time in dangerous ones—like those found at teen parties where drugs and alcohol are used.

4.9 We Have The Power To Change The Peer Pressure Dynamic

We should remember that adolescence is a period where our children regularly seek separation from us, but how deep this separation is and how long it lasts are largely dependent on how we act during it. This effort to separate and individuate is normal, and it does not represent our children's attempt to leave us forever—they are just trying to figure out who they are and what they want to become. If we stay true to our values while they explore new ones, we give them an emotional and ethical base to return to after time spent out in the storm of their everyday lives. If, however, we see their efforts as insults and affronts to us, we can react in ways that make our children doubt the strength of our commitment to them.

Dealing with a tempestuous, insulting, and dismissive teen on a daily basis can be exhausting; but as hard as it is, we must constantly try to remind ourselves what core issues are at play here: These are our children. We love them above all else. We do not want harm to befall them. We want a lasting, deep relationship with them when they are adults. They will grow out of this—adolescence is a phase, not a fixed state. They need us more than they know, and much more than they can admit. We cannot fail them.

If we remember this for the seemingly endless years adolescence lasts, we can find ourselves pleasantly surprised when one day, unexpectedly, our children treat us like human beings. In order for this to happen, though, we have to keep a steady hand; we have to stay true to our values when they are tested. By doing so, we demonstrate for our children how to live a life of character; and they will come to appreciate this more completely as they develop their own set of values and begin to live their lives according to those values. If we fail to do so, we set them adrift, we abandon them to the world of their peers; and if one thing is obvious above all else, it is that children with little or no skill at living their lives will never be able to show our children how to live theirs.

Ultimately, we have to realize peer pressure is not fixable; but it is certainly manageable. If we want to help our teens deal with it in their lives, we should first pay attention to how we deal with it in our lives.

One of the more common disappointments voiced by parents when they try to help their children deal with issues of acceptance is that their opinion does not matter anymore. When parents try to reassure their children that they are wonderful people, the response is usually along the lines of, "Well of course you think that—you're my parent!" When they try to lessen the impact of a situation by assuring their children that it will blow over or that it will not seem to matter as much after some time has passed, they are handed the ultimate dismissal in the form of, "You just don't get it!"

One of the best ways we can help our children deal with issues of peer pressure is to realize that a peer group influences everyone, and that we are not exempt. If we can recognize that peer pressure still exists in our lives and explore the ways we still fall prey to its power, we may be able to show our children that we actually do get it.

This can be difficult to do, because it requires that we be open to the idea that we care what other people think and honest about how we feel pressure to fit in. The problem most of us have when we think about how we succumb to or feel peer pressure is that it makes us feel shallow, and that isn't the way we want to see ourselves, so we block it out of our minds and don't think about it. Our kids, however, need us to think about it.

Realizing we are the victims of peer pressure is only the first step. If we want to help our children manage social pressure, we have to manage the way we act when we find ourselves victimized by the desire to fit in with our peers. It is not a crime to have a nice house or drive a nice car. It is, however, a terrible lesson to teach our children when we compromise our values or brutalize ourselves with debt to get these things in an effort to prove our worth to our peers. If we want to give our children the skills required to survive their world, we first must see if we are at least moderately capable of surviving ours.

Finally, we have to talk to our children about how all this feels. If we want our kids to think we actually do get it, we have to be able to put into words what it feels like for us to want to fit in; and we have to describe for them how we manage these pressures when we sense their presence. We must realize that the best way to teach our kids how to handle peer pressure is to model for them the skills we want them to learn. Showing them how to do it is massively more powerful than telling them how to do it and infinitely better than trying to convince them that it does not matter.

4.10 Some Final Thoughts On Peer Pressure

In the end, our children will be able to deal with peer pressure effectively only when they become comfortable in their own skins—when they view themselves as functional, capable and valuable. Since most peer pressure comes from within, it will only lose its power to influence our children's actions when they can find an emotional center of gravity based on their own worth. When they learn how to value themselves more than they value the opinions of their friends and classmates, they finally have the ability to escape the pull of peer influence.

We run into difficulty, however, when we expect our children to be able to do this while still in their teens; or that they will ever be able to do it completely. Too much of our discussion has been about how we as adults still deal with issues involving social pressure to not understand that this is something people struggle with throughout their lives; but we still must appreciate that teens are not going to be able to do this well most of the time. Adolescence is by definition a period of transition, a period of becoming; and it is unfair to expect a person on a journey simultaneously to complete that journey.

It is equally unfair to expect that you, in your role as parent, can magically fix this if you just perform a specific list of duties correctly; or to assume that if your child is currently struggling with issues involving peer pressure you have done something wrong. As we said earlier, this is not something you are going to fix; this is something your child will ultimately have to learn how to manage. This does not mean that we should not pay attention or that our efforts are meaningless; it just means that those efforts will only bear fruit over long periods. If you want to have an immediate impact on your child's life, turn to the section on what to do if your child is going to a party that day— those are suggestions you can implement immediately. When dealing with an issue like peer pressure, though, you need to take the long view or you are just going to end up frustrated and depressed.

The one thing we cannot allow ourselves to do is become discouraged when we encounter setbacks. Our children are counting on us to stay the course, even when they seem to be the ones trying to knock us off it. Remember, if you do not do the job, your child's peers will. That alone should be sufficient motivation to keep going even when things get overwhelming. We cannot abandon our children to their peers. It is not that they are bad kids; they are not. They just do not have the ability to guide our children well. We, however, do.

Part 5

Inside The Teenage Brain

5.1 What Are They Thinking?

If we distill the entirety of our interactions with parents into one all-inclusive theme, it is that they are desperately searching for answers: they want to know how to be better parents, how to keep their kids safe, how to help their teens grow up to be happy and healthy high-functioning adults. Most of all, they just want help understanding what is going on inside their kids' heads.

At a recent presentation we did for a group of parents in Las Vegas, Jonathan was describing the different styles of parenting when he noticed a woman in the audience who looked perplexed. When asked if she would like a quick recap of the last item, she just shook her head and said, "No, I'm OK with that. It's just that I have three teenage daughters at home, and each one of them is in full-blown bitch mode. I'm just trying to figure out if my style of parenting has anything to do with that." Judging by the reactions from the audience, she was far from alone—almost everyone in the room was either doubled over with laughter or nodding their heads ruefully as they thought about their own little nightmares waiting for them at home.

The bad news is that striving to implement a parenting style that will increase communication, lessen drug use, and create happy, healthy kids is commendable and recommended; but it probably won't result in an immediate reduction in the bitchiness scale. The good news is that there actually is an answer to the question of how to help your children succeed. If you want to understand what is going on inside your children's heads, you need to learn more about what is literally inside their heads—you need to understand their brains.

5.2   Weird Science—A New Look At Teen Brains

We are currently experiencing a sea change of information about what is actually happening inside our kids' brains. More importantly, we are getting clues about what that information means and how we can use it to be better parents, teachers, and mentors for our children. These miraculous new insights are possible due to a suite of cutting-edge scanning technologies that allow scientists to watch brains as they develop; but the even bigger magic happens when these techniques allow us to watch brains—in real time—as they work.

Over the past 20 years, this growing body of information has turned the scientific world on its head. Contrary to previous beliefs, we now know that brain formation does not end by the age of ten. Today, we have a new understanding: brains do not stop developing until the mid to late twenties; and even then, they have the capacity to change and improve in ways never before thought possible. This knowledge has a dark side, in that it shows there are very specific times when the brain is most capable of developing the skills needed for successful adult life. If those opportunities are missed it is very difficult—and sometimes impossible—to recapture them.

The importance of this cannot be overstated. The world is not kind to people who miss developmental opportunities. Both teens and young adults (and their parents) need to understand that they are laying down the foundation that will make them the adults they will become—they are building the house they will live in for the rest of their lives.

This is nothing short of a revolution; but it is also a revelation. Unfortunately, most parents have yet to utilize this information. In fact, it seems either many do not know of its existence or, if they do, they are so intimidated by the concept of 'brain science' that they shy away from it in the fear that they could not possibly understand or implement it. This goes beyond unfortunate and to us borders on tragic. There exists, right in front of us, information that has the power to change and improve lives, and yet we regularly fail to access or implement it. The time has come for that to change.

5.3 Can We Simplify Brain Science?

One of the promises we make as drug educators is that we will attempt to simplify a complex subject, and that is what we will attempt to do here also. While the terminology or concepts might appear to be unmanageable, if you commit yourself to reading the entire brain section at least once you will find that it all starts to make sense. We are going to do our best to keep this as user-friendly as possible. While we may run the risk of offending those of you among our readers who are neurobiologists, we will take that risk in the hope that we can make this information more easily accessible to the lay reader.

As you read, strive to remember what this information represents: it is one of the most powerful tools you have in your efforts to understand your children. It will not only educate you, it will also explain some of the more vexing issues parents face.

This information is manageable, and you will benefit beyond measure as you employ what you have learned. Just think—you are on the leading edge of a new era, a time when we will unlock secrets that have eluded us for millennia. This, to us, is beyond exciting—it is a game changer; and we all get to be a part of it if we just choose to.

5.4 The Miracle That Is The Brain

The human body starts out as just two cells, but at birth the brain will be made up of about 75-100 billion cells. Each of those 100 billion cells connect to other cells that surround them or work in concert with them—some estimates put the average number of connection points per brain cell at about 10,000, which means there are about one quadrillion points of contact between the cells in just one human brain. When you think about it for a moment, you will also understand that each of those connections can fire in different configurations; and that brings the realization that the possible number of different expressions of the human brain is staggeringly large. One estimate postulates that in a single human brain the possible number of different connection configurations exceeds the number of atoms in the known universe. If you are having trouble getting your head wrapped around these numbers, as most of us do, you start to appreciate the delicious irony of the human brain—it is so complex that it cannot understand itself!

The brain is a massive consumer of energy. Weighing in at just three pounds, the average brain comprises only 2.5-3% of the body's weight, and yet it consumes around 20% of the body's energy reserves. The brain's demand for oxygen is also quite dramatic. We can last weeks without food; days without water; but only about four minutes need to pass before a lack of oxygen causes brain damage or death. This becomes more important when we discuss how drugs and alcohol can depress respiration and realize the deadly consequences of vomiting while unconscious due to the effects of drugs or alcohol.

Most of the brain's work happens well outside our consciousness, and many times outside our control as well. Breathing, heart rate, digestion, waste management, and hormonal balance are all critical for our survival, but we actually have very little say about how the brain conducts that business. The part we do have control over though, is amazing. Everything we have ever created, learned, or realized about ourselves and the world we inhabit is a direct result of the conscious awareness that is our brain at work. Truly, this is one miraculous organ.

5.5 Your Teen's Brain Started At Square One

At birth, the brain is ready to perform or control some of the most basic tasks of survival—it helps the baby to eat, breathe, circulate blood, and eliminate waste. In essence, humans are born with the ability to survive as long as they receive their basic needs: food, air, water, and protection. This survival ability is genetically present without the action of outside forces.

In addition, we have other abilities as well, such as the ability to respond to language. This ability differs from survival, though, because it has the capacity to react to and change in response to the environment that surrounds it. One of the first and most powerful outside stimuli a baby experiences is the sound of its mother's voice, but how the baby's brain responds to that voice varies as criteria change. For example, language development typically follows a reasonably predictable arc in most children, but recent discoveries have shown that there is a significant delay if the baby's mother suffers from depression.

From this, we see that the potential for language exists at birth, but the expression of that potential is largely dependent upon exposure to distinct environmental influences. The salient point here is that its environment directly shapes the human brain, and the effects will be positive or negative as a direct result of those influences. Some factors—like drug and alcohol exposure during childhood and adolescence—can have devastating effects on how brains develop and function.

5.6 Windows Of Opportunity: Use It Or Lose It

As a baby survives and grows, its brain will continue to follow a predictable path of development, and that development occurs when certain parts of the brain prepare to come online. The process is realized when the parts of the brain that are ready to develop start to wildly increase the number of connections that exist in that region. In some cases, the number of connectors, called *dendrites*, will double in a short period. This rapid increase in connections, called *blossoming*, represents a dramatic period during which radical amounts of brain development can occur.

Since this blossoming makes brain development possible, we refer to this time as a *window of opportunity*. These periods are incredibly important, and if something interrupts or eliminates a window of opportunity the potential to develop a specific ability may be lost forever.

The reason these windows of opportunity are so critical is best understood in the context of the most important rule of brain development: If you use it, it will develop and grow stronger; if you do not use it, it will atrophy and be lost. This is the classic rule known to everyone who has ever gone to the gym or had a coach threaten: use it or lose it. This is where genetic potential and environmental influence mesh most powerfully. The newly created connections that are used will be stimulated and reinforced—they will grow stronger. Those that are not used will weaken or wither away in a process called *pruning*.

One of the more powerful examples of this is the development of vision in a newborn. If the nerves that carry the information gathered by the eyes to the brain (the optic nerves) are not stimulated regularly in the first few months of life, the ability to see may be lost forever. Animal experiments and occasional unlucky combinations of circumstances in humans have shown that depriving optic nerves of stimulation and use at certain critical times will result in blindness. There is nothing wrong with the eyes, and there is nothing wrong with the brain—the problem is that the two are no longer connected. In these cases, pruning of the optic nerve resulted because of a lack of regular stimulation from the environment. It was not used, so it was pruned, and vision was no longer possible.

5.7 Open Windows—When Drugs And Alcohol Devastate Teen Brains

It is critical to note that once the developmental period is successfully completed the nerve is no longer as threatened by periods of non-use. Thus, while a window of opportunity exists, there is a secondary influence at play called a *window of sensitivity*. Once a nerve wires, there is little risk it will unwire after the expiration of the window of sensitivity. You could take a child or an adult that has the ability to see and sequester them in a cave with no light for months at a time. Later, when they re-entered a lighted environment, after a period of readjustment, they would still possess the gift of sight. The window of sensitivity has passed. (Please do not throw your children into a cave, no matter how tempting that may sound at times. This is just an example.)

There is another aspect of the window of sensitivity that represents a different kind of danger: while the brain is developing during a window of opportunity, it is extremely vulnerable to damage if outside agents come into play. Substances that can potentially damage adult brains in large doses have the power to—in much smaller doses—profoundly damage the teenage brain during a window of sensitivity. The things your children do at parties as teenagers have the power to cause effects that last a lifetime—higher rates of alcoholism in adulthood, learning and memory problems, and deficits in skill development are just a few areas where this risk can play out.

Once the brain establishes the value of a connection through regular environmental stimulation, it will hard-wire and reinforce that connection by building a layer of insulation around the nerve. The insulation consists of a fatty material called *myelin*. When a nerve insulates, it becomes hugely more efficient at carrying information—100X faster than a non-insulated one. Unfortunately, research at the University of California, San Diego shows that even infrequent but ongoing alcohol use by teenagers can threaten this insulation and impair academic performance.

By far the most important thing to realize about all this blossoming and pruning and insulating and windows opening and closing is that they are all going on in your teenager's brain. Right now, as you read this sentence, these things are happening inside your teenager's head! Brains are not mature at age ten; and the regions that wait until adolescence, puberty and young adulthood to mature are some of the most powerful at influencing behavior. They are also some of the most susceptible to damage from substance use—right at the very time when your kids are most likely to consider the inception of use.

When you begin to understand what brain sections develop last—and how those brain regions affect your children's ability to make good choices—you'll be able to parent in ways that allow for the development of skills and abilities while simultaneously doing what you can to keep your kids safe in complex social situations.

5.8 Are You Sure My Teen Has All Three?

The brain consists of three main sections: the ***brain stem*** (also called the reptile brain), the ***limbic area***, and the ***cortex***.

The brain stem is largely responsible for regulating that which we have little conscious control over: breathing, heartbeat, body temperature, and reflex actions. Since it is mostly beyond conscious influence, we tend to ignore it a lot of the time. The brain stem becomes more meaningful, though, when large doses of drugs or alcohol start to shut down its functions. This is when breathing slows and becomes shallow and irregular; it is also when heart rate and body temperature start to fall. At this point, if a child does not receive emergency care from an EMT or a doctor, there is a distinct possibility he or she may die.

The limbic area is mostly associated with the emotional aspects of our being, but it is also the area responsible for the fight/flight/freeze response to threats and is the seat of memory formation and learning. This area will come powerfully into play in our discussions about teenagers' volatile emotions, but we will also explore how environmental factors like drugs, alcohol and stress influence the function of structures in this area.

The cortex is the brain region most closely associated with our humanity. It is where we conduct the business of thought and consciousness—planning, reasoning, morals, inhibition control, and recognizing consequences that occur because of actions. For our purposes, one area of the cortex will occupy most of our attention—it's the area right behind our foreheads called the ***prefrontal cortex***, which we will refer to from now on as the ***PFC***.

5.9 So That's Why My Teen Is Impulsive, Forgetful, And Makes Decisions Like A Four-Year-Old!

The PFC is one of the last areas of the brain to achieve maturity, and it weighs heavily in our understanding of our teenagers' actions. When it finally reaches full function, it conducts the business of inhibition, impulse control, planning, and problem solving. It is also responsible for decision-making, risk measurement, stress regulation, working memory, and the ability to read emotions, especially the emotions observed in facial expressions. The PFC links cause and effect—it is the part of the brain that, if it is working as it should, screams "STOP!" when a person is about to do something fabulously stupid. Obviously, a brain that lacks the full ability to do all of these important jobs is a brain that can get a teenager into a load of trouble before he or she even realizes a threat exists.

As we noted earlier, the PFC experiences a dramatic period of blossoming and pruning from the teen years into early adulthood. Because this area is so closely associated with impulse control, a lack of development here means that teens have a serious lack of ability to control urges, resist temptation, and manage risk. We are going to spend a good amount of time exploring how this can affect your day-to-day dealings with your teen children and how it can dramatically affect the decisions they make in high stress social situations—like parties.

Let's return for a moment to the limbic region, for it is there that we find a number of important brain areas that can have a powerful influence over not only how your children act and respond to emotion, but also dictate how well they form memories and learn.

One of the most pivotal structures in the limbic area is the *hippocampus*, a small bilateral (mirrored structures, one on each side of the brain) area that is the focal point for memory formation. Not only does it act as a repository for certain types of memory, the hippocampus is also the clearinghouse and the arbiter of where memory is to be stored. When hippocampal function is impaired, memory and learning suffer. Unfortunately, many factors affect the hippocampus; and of particular interest to us is that not only do stress and hormonal activity affect it, alcohol and drugs do as well.

We should note that the hippocampi in teens who abuse alcohol are smaller than those who do not; and even though brain size does not directly relate to brainpower, diminished size caused by drug and alcohol use does seem to affect hippocampal function in teens.

5.10 Why Teens Act Before They Think

Another important structure in the limbic area is the *amygdala*, an almond shaped nugget buried deep in the brain that is responsible for our almost instantaneous reaction to danger. The amygdala is what causes the cascade of physical reactions that lead to the fight/flight/freeze reaction in the face of danger.

This classic fight or flight response is what prepares us to directly engage or flee from enemies or predators; and while that has served to increase our survival potential for eons, it can be the source of great distress as we struggle to deal with the emotional outbursts to which teens can be so prone. One of the more unfortunate aspects of teenagers having underdeveloped PFC's is that instead of analyzing facial expressions for emotional content the way adults do—with the PFC—a teen is more likely to respond with the amygdala. Since it is essentially a threat response center, it is not hard to see how many non-threatening facial expressions might be seen as threats when processed via the amygdala.

It also pays to remember that the amygdala's success lies in the fact that it can get us out of the way of danger quickly. When we respond via the amygdala, we can actually start down a path of reaction to a perceived threat well before we have had any time to analyze the true nature of the threat—or if the danger is even real. When the amygdala is running the show, we literally act before we think.

5.11 Why Does This Matter?

When our children respond to something we say in a manner that seems far removed from sanity, it helps to remember what they may actually be doing is responding to directives handed down from the amygdala. We did not intend what we said as a threat, but our children may perceive it as such, and they respond in a manner that fits the way they see the situation.

Parents have to remember not to fall prey to the amygdala misread. When your child accuses you of a particular agenda ("Why do you always treat me like I'm three years old!?") it is incumbent upon you, as the adult with the fully functioning PFC, to patiently reframe the conversation. Instead of yelling back at your child, it will be more proactive to say, for example, "I'm sorry. That's not what I meant to imply. I just get frustrated when you leave wet towels all over the floor after you get ready for school. How about this: you try harder to pick up your towels; I'll try harder to communicate more clearly. OK?"

This does not mean you always have to walk on eggshells, and it does not mean you have to suffer constant verbal abuse by your teens, but it does mean you owe it to yourself and your children not to take the bait. It falls to you not to escalate a very common and predictable event into a conflagration by becoming offended when your children suffer amygdala-based emotional misreads. When your teen is reacting to an encounter with you in what seems to be a completely unreasonable fashion, before you respond in kind, ask yourself, "Is there any way they could have perceived what I said as threatening, accusatory, or fear inspiring?" Remember, you have to try to look at it from their perspective—you cannot just look at it through the lens of your intentions. It is not what you meant; it is what they heard that matters.

Low functioning PFC's and hair-trigger amygdalae are not the only reasons teens regularly misread emotions. We can reframe the primary rule of brain development—use it or lose it—and instead say, "What you practice, you get better at." This approach provides insight into why teens are more likely than adults are to misread emotions: they have not had as much practice at it. As we said in the opening paragraphs of this section, it is a lot easier to give children the benefit of the doubt when we have insight into how they are seeing a situation and how brain development (or lack thereof) can dramatically affect how they behave.

There is one last thing to note about the amygdala and how it functions: it is an area where emotional memories are stored, and it may play a major role in repeat drug use. The amygdala can recall the tone and quality of emotional experiences; so if the brain receives a particularly pleasant jolt from a dose of drugs, when the intensity of the drug high wanes it may be the emotional memories stored in the amygdala that say, "Hey! Do that again!"

5.12 One Final Note On Brain Regions

We all have stress in our lives, and one of the basic rules of stress is this: You are going to deal with it. You may do it in a healthy way, or you may do it in an unhealthy way, but you are going to deal with it. One thing we should note about teens is that they are at a point where they are experiencing a lot of stress from school, parents, peers, romance, not enough sleep, self-doubt, and on and on and on. Years ago, a manager Jonathan had when he worked at Legal Sea Foods spoke about why it is so stressful to be a waiter: lots of responsibility, little or no authority or power. We cannot imagine that there is a more accurate description of what being a teenager is like—lots of responsibility, little or no authority or power. This can result in a condition of chronic stress.

Chronic stress is highly taxing on brain function, emotional well-being, and the immune system. Unfortunately for teens, stress management is handled in large part by the PFC, and we have already spoken of the developmental level teenagers' PFC's occupy. It's not much of a wonder, then, since teens lack the brain power to adequately deal with stress, to see them reaching for a drink or a drug as a quick fix for their chronic stress. What teens do not have the ability and experience to recognize is that not only does drug and alcohol use result in a net stress gain in their lives, but that very use often leads to increased deficits in brain performance that can cause even more difficulty dealing with stress down the road. Using drugs and alcohol to mitigate teen stress is a recipe for disaster.

5.13 The Computer Brain

One way to look at the brain is to compare it to a computer. The physical brain itself is essentially the hard drive: it stores information and is the physical framework over which that information must travel when we access or use it. The mind is the software and the memory: it is the contents of that stored information as well as the directions on what to do and how to do it. All this information in the brain is stored and moved about much as it is in a computer—it is nothing more than a series of electrical impulses. Therefore, the brain is a biological instrument that runs on electricity and the computer is a technological instrument that runs on electricity.

There is one huge difference between the two: The computer is able to relay its electric signals from one area to the next because there is an unbroken circuit stretching from the area of origin to the area of delivery. If the tiniest gap exists in the circuit, it will not work. The brain, on the other hand, is full of gaps. In fact, cells in the brain never touch in the areas where communication occurs—there is always a gap between two cells trying to speak to each other. These gaps are called *synapses*, and if the brain is to work, it must find a way to bridge the synaptic gap. This bridging relies on brain chemicals called *neurotransmitters*, and their function is one of the more fascinating and potentially frightening aspects of brain science.

5.14 Brain Chemicals: A Double-Edged Sword

When the brain moves information, the cell delivering the message fires off an electrical pulse when it reaches what is called an *action potential*. Brain cells do not ever 'kind of' fire—they are on or they are off. When it reaches action potential, the cell transmits an electrical pulse. However, if any communication is to occur, that pulse must make it to the next cell—it has to deliver its message. It has a problem doing so electrically because of the gap—the synapse. Electricity does not effectively transition across gaps. What happens next is amazing: the electric pulse inspires the cell delivering the message to release a burst of chemical messengers—the neurotransmitters we mentioned earlier. These chemical messengers are looking for a place to park, and they find it on the next cell when they arrive at structures called *receptors*. When a neurotransmitter arrives at a cell that can accept it, it fits into the receptor as a piece fits into a puzzle—and the message is delivered. Every thought humans have ever had, every action we have ever taken, every word ever spoken, and every emotion ever felt has been the result of electrical pulses and chemical messengers conducting the business of the brain. It is a system of amazing function, and when it works as designed, it can result in miraculous feats. When it underperforms or when outside forces alter its functions—as in the case of drug and alcohol abuse or use by teenagers—the results can be disastrous.

Although scientists have found that there are about 100 neurotransmitters at work in the brain, we are only going to focus on two: *dopamine* and *serotonin*. Others, like glutamate, norepinephrine and gamma amino butyric acid (GABA) are also important, but for our purposes, we most need to understand dopamine and serotonin.

5.15 Neurotransmitters 101—Pleasure And Mood

Basic brain science says that dopamine is the brain's feel-good chemical. If you have ever experienced a jolt of pleasure, you got that jolt from dopamine. Dopamine plays a critical role in human survival—it rewards behaviors that make us survive at higher rates or those that insure the continuation of the species. When we get hungry, we seek food; and when we eat food, we get a jolt of dopamine pleasure in our brains. Thirsty people get dopamine pleasure when they drink water. We also get a sizeable helping of dopamine pleasure when we attempt to reproduce, an action that is pretty critical for the survival of the species! Interestingly, dopamine also surges in teenagers' brains when they experience new situations and when they take risks, something we will explore later.

Another facet of what dopamine does to affect human behavior concerns the notion that we are most likely to repeat two types of activities: those that inspire pleasure and those that reduce or eliminate pain. It is easy to see, then, that when dopamine responses are awakened or enhanced by the use of drugs and alcohol, that use will probably be repeated.

Dopamine takes on a more sinister hue when viewed through this lens. It is the main reason why people return to a drug after their first use—they have awakened a powerful and repeatable way to receive pleasure at levels hard to achieve through any other method. Dopamine then becomes not just a messenger of pleasure; it also becomes a catalyst capable of establishing drug abuse and addiction. In fact, all drugs of addiction awaken this dopamine reward system. This becomes more ominous when we realize that teens and young adults are particularly sensitive to dopamine-based rewards.

The other neurotransmitter we need to discuss is serotonin, often referred to as the mood stabilizing brain chemical. Anything that influences the amount of serotonin present in the brain or how the brain responds to different levels can result in dramatic mood swings in teens. One way to think about the role serotonin plays is to notice that a major segment of the antidepressant market consists of drugs called selective serotonin reuptake inhibitors (SSRI's). These drugs reduce the rate at which the brain reabsorbs serotonin after it enters the gaps between cells in the brain—the synapses. Since the SSRI's ensure that the serotonin stays active longer, its effects are more pronounced and the person's mood is more elevated than it would have been without the drugs.

Changes that result from young girls entering puberty and starting their menstrual cycles can play havoc on the levels of dopamine and serotonin present in their brains at any given time. These wild fluctuations are the primary reason why you may have a daughter who is singing show tunes one minute and dirges the next; and it may also be one of the reasons young women experience depression at a markedly higher rate after they enter puberty. There is ample evidence too that some drugs of abuse, notably ecstasy and methamphetamine, can radically alter the amounts of serotonin present and negatively affect the brain's ability to utilize the chemical when it is present.

Parents can dramatically improve the relationships they have with their children if they possess a basic understanding of the powerful effects these two neurotransmitters can have on teenagers' behaviors. They can double that influence if they appreciate the devastating effects drugs and alcohol can have on how neurotransmitters function or fail in teen brains and then parent in ways that limit their children's exposure to environments that encourage drug and alcohol use.

5.16 Teens And Hormones: Duck And Run For Cover

One of the profound influences teen brains find themselves overwhelmed by is the increase in the production of hormones during puberty. We are all familiar with the big players—*testosterone* and *estrogen*—and we will focus our attention on these. Most parents know that their teen sons are changing into men—it's happening in front of their eyes—but those same parents may not know that their son's testosterone levels are rocketing up by as much as tenfold numerous times each day. It does not take a lot of imagination to picture what effect that might have on a young man's predisposition to try to impress girls, challenge other males, bristle at attempts to invade his personal space, fall prey to impulse, and seek risky behavior.

It turns out that the amygdala is saturated with receptor sites for testosterone. This means that if you are unlucky enough to have an even slightly challenging encounter with a male teen who happens to be in the throes of a testosterone spike, the results can be baffling for both of you. It's hard to realize, when your son is screaming at you to get your hands off his stuff, that he really doesn't understand why he is so protective of his possessions at that moment—he just is. He is as much a victim of that testosterone spike as you are, but unfortunately, it puts you on the receiving end of his abuse and can lead you to feel disrespected or threatened. It is easier to deal with this situation calmly if you realize what is causing it and how little it actually has to do with the quality of the relationship you thought you had with your son—you know, before he started screaming at you.

Parents of girls can certainly see the effects of estrogen on their daughters' physical appearance. Unfortunately, many are not aware of how the interplay between estrogen other hormones and brain chemicals can cause rapid and dramatic mood changes and influence a susceptibility to depression. Lest we lose all hope, it is important to note that hormonal fluctuations in teen girls also cause a spike in how much dopamine is present in the hippocampus, an effect that makes them more likely, in the short term, to succeed at a higher rate academically than males will.

One important aspect parents have to realize about puberty is that it marks the time when their children start to think about sex and relationships with their peers. Male teenagers go through periods when they think about sex a lot. Mom—if you want to know how much your son is thinking about sex, just picture what level of sexual thought in your son's mind would make you feel a bit uncomfortable—now multiply that by about 100, and you are probably close.

If your child is female, she may not thinking about sex with the same frequency or intensity that a male child would, but she is certainly centering her attention and energy on relationships, both with her female peers and the boys she regularly deals with. The different levels of importance men and women assign to sex and relationships can lead to serious confusion about what each party wants to get from any interactions they may have; and the chaotic environment present at teenage parties can increase the levels of confusion to dangerous levels if drugs and alcohol are present.

It is important to note that this search for relationships and sex meshes perfectly with the novelty-seeking behavior we said could raise teen dopamine levels. This can also explain a lot of teens' tendency to draw away from their parents and migrate toward the company of other teens. Who would want to spend time with their parents (predictable and boring) instead of their peers (new and exciting), given the choice? The very act of seeking or pondering new relationships is exciting and motivates kids to put themselves out there in ways they never thought possible even a few years before.

Unfortunately, puberty happens at increasingly younger ages than it did even a few hundred years ago. We realize that 200 years sounds like a long time, but it is no more than the blink of a eye when we're talking about the kind of changes that have resulted in the onset of puberty falling by more than 5 years in that period. What used to happen at 17 or 18 is now happening at 11 or 12—and even earlier in some cases! The problem is that if puberty happens at such a young age, the PFC's of those kids are not even close to being able to handle the task of assessing the risk of sexual activity (i.e., the possibility that their actions could result in pregnancy or the transmission of disease). It is frightening for parents to realize that at the very time when their children are least able to deal with the impulse to take all kinds of risks, their brains are being battered by a chemical stew of hormones and neurotransmitters that increase the likelihood of risk-taking behavior.

5.17   Seeking Sensation And Taking Risks—Where Did My Teen's Brain Go?

Occasionally we have the unfortunate privilege of ringside seats to teenage decision-making disasters. Whether it is a group of students found smoking marijuana on school property or a student caught selling drugs on campus isn't really important. What matters is that we have seen some of the smartest, luckiest, most pampered kids on the planet do things that seem to indicate they have lost their minds. Yet that cannot be what is happening—there must be some other explanation for why amazingly intelligent young people do things that make it look like the switch that powers their brains has been set to the off position.

What we must realize is that decision making in teenagers has very little to do with how intelligent they are. Their ability to choose one behavior over another is hampered by the almost perfect lack of function in some areas of their PFC's, and that lack of function is particularly notable in the areas of sensation seeking, perceived risk, and the consequences that might befall a person exhibiting such behaviors. A teenager can be simultaneously very mature intellectually while still being almost completely blind to how a particular choice or behavior will affect them in the future. We do ourselves no favors if we assume that our children's academic prowess in any way carries over into their ability to make good behavioral choices.

A few years ago, a headmaster we know recounted a story about an experience he had with one of his students. One day after school, he was sitting at his desk when he happened to look out a window in his office that faced the street. As his gaze drifted to a telephone pole in front of the school, he was surprised to see what he described as a "very recognizable male ponytail sticking out from behind one side of the pole and a joint sticking out from behind the other side of the pole." Confronted with the circumstance of one of his students obviously smoking marijuana in front of the school, he knew he had to do something, so he got up, went out, and dragged the kid back into his office.

He continued, "Now, I knew better than to even ask the question, but I couldn't stop myself, so I said, 'What were you thinking?'" Without missing a beat, the young man looked back at him and said, "If I knew that, I wouldn't be here right now!" The astonishing poetry of that answer couldn't highlight the problem any more clearly—he was there because of his almost complete inability to see beyond his actions; and he couldn't see beyond his actions because the part of his brain that does that work—the prefrontal cortex—just wasn't up to speed yet.

5.18 What Were You Thinking?

We don't know if the parent exists who has not asked the same question of his or her own children—"What were you thinking!?" Unfortunately, and yet completely understandably (once you know what's going on inside a teenage brain), there really isn't an answer to that question that will satisfy an adult, especially in light of the circumstances under which it normally has to be asked. The answer, of course, is not that they were not thinking; it is just that they were not thinking about the same things an adult would be thinking about in a similar situation. The reason for that is deeply rooted in the differences between how an adult brain sees the world and how a teenage brain sees the world; and it has very little to do with choosing not to think and everything to do with how we perceive risk and reward at different times in our lives.

One of the hardest things to do with our adult brains is realize how perfectly suited teenage brains are for the work that is laid before them. Think about the biological mandates they face: Leave home. Find a mate. Find food. Find shelter. Protect what is theirs. All of these require teens to take risks, explore new worlds, and develop new relationships. None of these is going to happen by sitting around the cave staring at pictures of bison on the walls—teenagers have to head out into the world, seek new experiences, and above all, take risks. It would seem, then, that risk taking is a behavior that must be richly rewarded, since it is an evolutionary necessity—a survival skill.

How does this pertain to today's teenagers—the ones with the rooms of their own, so much food that childhood obesity is now a health epidemic, college dorm rooms waiting for them, house parties galore, text messaging, and social media pages boasting of friends numbering in the hundreds, if not the thousands? Well, it does not seem to pertain to them at all, until we realize that what evolution has wrought is not undone quickly. A few hundred years of technological development and economic prosperity do not come close to erasing what is deeply etched into our DNA. We must understand that behaviors related to survival—the most important job we have—are more deeply seated than any others are.

5.19 Parties And Teens: Perfect Match Or Perfect Storm?

Recall what we said in the section on dopamine: survival behaviors are rewarded with jolts of pleasure. It is not too big a leap to understand that teenagers get pleasure when they experience new situations, meet new people (especially ones that are sexually attractive!), and take risks. It is an absolute fact that teens experience increases in dopamine when they are in novel situations. They get an even bigger dose of dopamine when they develop relationships that have sexual overtones. In addition, they get a jolt of pleasure when they experience situation rich with risk. We must remember that whenever a behavior is rewarded with a dose of pleasure, it is not going to happen just once—that behavior is going to be repeated.

Parents need to understand the attraction teen parties hold: they offer all of these elements in one neat package. Novel situations abound, members of the opposite sex are legion, and risk waits around every corner. When our teenagers ask us if they can go to a party, we need to keep in mind that they may as well, in their view of things, be asking, "May I please survive?" Remember, though, that they are not consciously using this to manipulate you. They may not even be aware why it is that they are so desperately invested in getting permission to go to the party—they just know it feels like this party is a matter of life or death.

Unfortunately, there are many land mines waiting for an eager teenager seeking sensation in today's world. When we say that novel situations result in dopamine spikes, we have to realize that teens are bound to see any new situation as attractive; and that they often seek new experiences solely because they are new. Since they are not very good at predicting what consequences might result from their actions, new situations can deteriorate rapidly. Instead of taking a moment to figure out if a new behavior will result in a good outcome or a poor one, teenagers will generally jump feet first and wait until later to assess the quality of the results.

5.20 Do Teens Have Enough Free Time To Learn How To Make Good Choices?

Another difficulty is that we have done a good job of filling up our kids' days with all kinds of responsibilities and obligations—most of the students we work with are college-bound, and the activities required of a teenager on that path consume most of their waking hours. While this may be good in one sense, it also means there are fewer safe risk options available to our teens. The little free time they do have can sometimes offer few risk-taking opportunities beyond drugs, alcohol, and sex—in other words, parties. We must remember that when teens use drugs and alcohol, they can fall prey to the effects those drugs have on brain function. A teen under the influence of alcohol is less inhibited, less fearful, less reasonable, less committed to his or her normal moral code, has poorer judgment, and can sometimes experience spikes in aggression. In other words, a teen that normally would be very unlikely to take untoward risks can almost instantly become a high-level risk taker just because of the presence of alcohol in the body. You cannot assume that the child you know so well at home will act normally or predictably once he or she arrives at a party where drugs and alcohol are available and social pressure dictates that the way to gain acceptance is to use them.

5.21 Risk Taking Through The Eyes Of A Teen

One aspect of risk taking that is regularly misunderstood is the way teens see risk. One of the most commonly cited teen truths is that they think they are immortal. Actually, they do not. Teens regularly overestimate the risk of lung cancer for cigarette smokers, yet they still smoke at disturbingly high levels. Recent drops in teen smoking are the result of a number of different factors (e.g. price sensitivity, anti-tobacco ads that demonize tobacco companies) but they did not happen because those teens suddenly became afraid of lung cancer. The unacceptable percentage of teens that still smoke do so because, while they are conscious of the risks associated with smoking, they are more motivated by the rewards these types of risky behaviors carry with them.

It may be hard to understand what rewards a teen would gain from smoking until you see the perceived benefits cigarette use offers young people. Primarily, they see smoking as an adult behavior. Teens that smoke may also see themselves as rebels and revel in the experience of flaunting adult authority. The brand of cigarette a teen chooses to smoke can also speak volumes about what type of person they want others to think they are—we regularly speak in our classrooms about the disingenuous nature of cigarette advertisements that tout their sponsor's commitment to "sustainable agricultural practices" and herald the organic nature of their tobacco. Cigarettes have the power to offer young people identity, and that is a huge part of what they are searching for. In other words, teens do not think they are immortal; they just value the rewards drugs seem to offer more than they fear the risks. These perceived rewards can be powerful motivators for the use of alcohol and drugs as well, and the potential costs teenagers incur via the use of alcohol and drugs cannot be overstated.

5.22 Alcohol And Drugs: Not A Rite Of Passage; Rather, A Bell Tolling

One of the ways we see parents navigate the issue of drug and alcohol use is for them to recall what they did when they were young and assume that as long as their kids don't do anything worse, they will probably turn out OK. This does not represent the entirety, of course, but parents who have essentially given up regularly surprise us. We are still amazed by the frequent claim, "They're all going to drink or get high sooner or later—why don't we just figure out how they can do it safely?" Well, for a number of reasons, actually. First, as the title of our first book says, not all kids do drugs. Second, one of the best ways to make sure your children do end up drinking and drugging is to assume that they will—when you stop expecting it to happen, then the possibility it will happen automatically goes down. Finally, and most importantly, the idea that we can somehow teach our kids to do drugs or drink alcohol safely is a fairytale.

New studies indicate that parents who try to teach their children to drink alcohol safely and parents who drink with their kids in an effort to teach moderation are doomed to failure. Instead of achieving safety and moderation, their kids are more likely to abuse alcohol, more likely to struggle in school, and more likely to be victims of alcoholism as adults. With each passing day, our new understanding of the teen brain increasingly indicates that it is no longer possible to use the words "teen use" and "safe use" in the same sentence. Since their brains are at a point where they are easily open to damage, we now understand that teen drug and alcohol use is a direct threat to their physical health and mental well-being.

Parents who think they can teach their children to drink safely (if they can just create a situation where the teens can practice moderate drinking) are convinced that what they are doing is rational. Often, in an effort to justify their actions, they will try to employ some of the same brain rules we have talked about. If teens get better at what they do regularly, why can't regular, controlled drinking around adults teach them how to drink safely? Unfortunately, there is some confusion over the words "better at" and "grows stronger." The sad truth is that regular use of alcohol does not teach teens how to drink safely; it teaches them how to drink regularly. They do not get better at drinking safely—that is a physical impossibility—they just get better at drinking.

The other problem we have to come to terms with is exactly what developmental message is delivered to a teen brain when a child regularly infuses it with alcohol. A brain that is exposed to alcohol in this manner will quickly start to adapt to the presence of that alcohol—it has to develop in such a way as to incorporate the presence of alcohol into its operating system. Unfortunately, these changes may make the brain think it cannot operate without alcohol in the future.

Teens who drink alcohol regularly have a much higher risk of alcoholism in adulthood, and other drugs show similar patterns of a heightened risk of addiction following teen use. Alcohol use by teens has a more pronounced negative effect on memory and learning than a similar dose would in an adult. These memory deficits directly affect academic performance, and they may last for a lifetime.

Teen drinking results in a diminishment in hippocampal size in teens. Evidence exists that after heavy alcohol use—such as what teens experience during spring break style binges—the cells in the hippocampus die off at an astronomical rate when the flow of alcohol ceases, and these damaging effects may never repair themselves.

Adolescents do not get sleepy when they drink, nor do the slur their words or experience the coordination deficits as early as adults do when they drink. Because of this, teen drinkers frequently underestimate how drunk they are and continue to drink well past the point where they do damage to their brains. They are also more likely to attempt things they now have no ability to do safely, like drive a car or make decisions about sexual activity.

Teen brains experience damage from alcohol use in doses that would not harm an adult brain. Remember, teen brains are deep in the process of blossoming and pruning, and because of this, they are extremely sensitive to damage caused by drug and alcohol use during this time.

In addition to these threats, any activity that has the potential to increase dopamine production or availability results in the brain cutting back on the amount of dopamine normally available in the tissues over time. This lack of dopamine leaves teens feeling terrible, and motivates them to seek out things that will temporarily but quickly provide a dopamine boost, which usually means reaching for another drink or drug. Of course, when this dose wears off they are left feeling worse than ever, whereupon they repeat the process. This feedback spiral can progress very quickly in some teens. In others, it is more subtle; but it is never good for the long-term health and safety of their brains.

Unbelievably, we still get an alarming amount of pushback on this subject. Not a month goes by that a parent does not question our stance on the issue of providing alcohol to teens at home and at parent-sponsored parties in an effort to keep them safe. In 2012, a TV reporter in the Washington, D.C. area left the air for a short period because of threats she and her children received when she ran a series of reports on underage alcohol use. We should note that the threats and abuse did not just come from underage drinkers. One parent wrote in a Facebook post, "You can't try and take away something that teens love without retaliation. Haven't you ever heard of teenage rebellion? Teens love to drink and I'm sure they'll be laughing it up about your report while they party tonight."

We need to put this dusty, old, outdated thought process where it belongs—out back, in the bin with "The earth is flat" and "I think there is a world market for maybe five computers."

We have better information now than we did in the past about how drugs and alcohol damage and alter teen brain development. We owe it to our children to make decisions based on this new knowledge, especially if decisions based on the old information are dangerous.

As bad as alcohol is for teen brains, other drugs do them no favors either. Nicotine use is associated with a drop in serotonin, and we know from our discussion of brain chemicals that cannot be good. Smokers who start in their teens become much more deeply addicted to tobacco than smokers who start as adults do. Unfortunately, almost all smokers start when they are teens. Nicotine is one of the only drugs that can cause the brain to create more receptor sites for it to occupy, and this effect is more evident in teens. With each new receptor site created, craving for nicotine goes up and the addiction becomes more powerful. Teens who smoke run a serious risk of addiction and all the disastrous health consequences associated with tobacco use. Yet because their brains are so ill equipped to understand the price of this decision, they end up starting smoking anyway.

When you read the sections in this book that detail the current risks associated with each different type of drug, it quickly becomes apparent that we have a direct obligation to our children to do whatever is in our power to protect their brains from drug and alcohol exposure. We finally have to realize that stories about how "I drank and did drugs in high school, and I turned out fine!" are just that—stories. When our children's safety and well-being are on the line, anecdotes do not carry any water. We need to pay attention to the science; and the science says teens, alcohol, and drugs do not mix.

Part 6

The Dangers And Costs

One of the most frustrating aspects of teen drug and alcohol use at parties is that, unless there is an immediate disaster as a result, it goes ignored and underappreciated in the ways it affects the lives of those teens. It is hard to see that an adult life destroyed by alcoholism that resulted from teen use is as heartbreaking as a life shattered by a car accident caused by a teen driving drunk. Until we learn to see that both are often the result of teen drug and alcohol use at parties, we will continue to pay these seemingly invisible long-term costs.

In this section, we will outline some of the most powerful short and long-term consequences that teen drug and alcohol use can cause. We will break them down by topic—some sections pertain to the drug used; others will address the associated risks that their use can cause.

6.1 Alcohol

- 47% of 14-year-olds who drink regularly will be alcoholics as adults, compared to just 9% of those who start their regular use at 21 or older.

- More than 90% of the alcohol consumed by teens is done so by binge drinking.

- On any given day, over 11,000 teenagers take their first drink.

- Alcohol is the cause of 60% of all teen deaths in car accidents.

- Over 40% of all drunken driving fatalities involve teenagers.

- There were 522 underage DUI arrests in one year that involved teens below 14 years of age. An amazing 113 of these 522 cases involved *kids who were 10 years old or younger*.

- In 2010, 65.2% of high school seniors had consumed alcohol at least once in the past year; 44% reported being drunk in the past year.

- Alcohol plays a role in over 300 teen suicides each year.

- Almost 75% of teen drinkers drink at parties hosted by other teens.

- Teens who binge drink are 3 times more likely to binge drink as adults.

- Occasional heavy drinking—also known as party use—causes damage to adolescent brains in very specific areas related to academic function. "The magnitude of the difference is 10 percent. I like to think of it as the difference between an A and a B," reported Susan Tapert, the UCSD professor conducting the research.

- New studies from 2011 report that damage to the brains of binge drinking teens and young adults results in cortical

147

thinning in the pre-frontal cortex. Damage to this section of the brain can harm cognitive functions such as paying attention, controlling impulses that lead to irrational behavior, planning, and making decisions. It can also impair prospective memory, which is the ability to remember to carry out an activity at some future point, such as doing homework or going to the dentist.

6.2 Marijuana

- One in six people who start using marijuana as adolescents become addicted.

- A 2012 article about an extensive longitudinal study done over a period of 38 years revealed that chronic, long-term, dependent marijuana use that started in adolescence resulted in an average loss of 8 points in IQ. A Duke University researcher, Madeline Meier, noted that: (1) the key variable is the age at which the use started; (2) the loss did not appear to reverse after the use ceased; and (3) "Marijuana is not harmless, particularly for adolescents." As we noted earlier, there is a heightened vulnerability to long-term brain changes when drug use starts in the early to middle teens. These changes can lead to higher levels of dependency, addiction, and cognitive problems. This new study highlights another area of risk long suspected and now observed: diminished intelligence.

- Low doses of THC (delta-9 tetrahydrocannabinol, the principal active ingredient in marijuana) moderately impair cognitive and psychomotor tasks associated with driving; and marijuana users experience severe driving impairment because of high doses, chronic use, and use in combination with low doses of alcohol. The more difficult and unpredictable the task, the more likely marijuana will impair performance.

- Cannabis use during adolescence and young adulthood increases the risk of psychotic symptoms.

- Cannabis use appears to be associated with an earlier onset of psychotic illness.

- New research shows that people who start using marijuana at a young age and those who use the greatest amount of marijuana may be the most cognitively impaired. "...marijuana use has a direct effect on executive function, and both age of onset and magnitude of marijuana use can significantly influence cognitive processing," according to Staci Gruber, PhD, at McLean Hospital and Harvard Medical School.

- Recent research challenges the increasingly popular belief that smoking marijuana is less harmful to health than smoking tobacco. Researchers in Canada report that smoking marijuana, like smoking tobacco, has toxic effects on cells. Marijuana smoke caused significantly more damage to cells and DNA than tobacco smoke, the researchers note.

- A 2008 study finds that the development of bullous lung disease occurs in marijuana smokers approximately 20 years earlier than in tobacco smokers. The inhalation style of marijuana smokers increases the deposition of particulate matter in the lung that results in greater and faster destruction of lung tissue.

- PET scans of regular marijuana users show that marijuana may continue to affect the brain three or more days after use, particularly affecting motor coordination, memory and learning.

6.3 Pharmaceutical Drugs

- Opiates, sedatives, tranquilizers, and stimulants are addictive when abused.

- Six of the top 10 illicit drugs abused by 12th-graders in 2009 consisted of those prescribed or purchased over the counter.

- A 2011 LA Times analysis of CDC (the Center for Disease Control, an arm of the federal government) data revealed that prescription drug overdose deaths outnumbered those caused by car crashes.

- The same LA Times article noted that prescription drugs caused one death every 14 minutes in the US in 2009.

- In 2009, the CDC reported that 1 in 5 high school students in the United States have abused prescription drugs, including the opioid painkillers OxyContin, Percocet, and Vicodin.

- Hospital emergency room visits involving nonmedical use of prescription narcotic pain relievers have more than doubled, rising 111 percent between 2004 and 2008.

- One in four 18-25 year olds will abuse prescription painkillers in their lifetimes.

- "The scope of the problem is vast—opioid overdose is now the second leading cause of accidental death in the United States and the prevalence (of abuse) is second only to marijuana," said Thomas McLellan, PhD; Director of the new Center for Substance Abuse Solutions at the University Of Pennsylvania School Of Medicine.

- Animal studies indicate female adolescents who abuse opiates may predispose their children and grandchildren to addiction.

- Adolescent brains exposed to the painkiller OxyContin can sustain lifelong and permanent changes in their reward systems, leading to future likelihood of addiction.

- From 1998 to 2005, calls to poison control centers for ADHD medication abuse almost doubled, with Adderall being the biggest driver of the change.

6.4 Assault, Addiction, Violence, Injury, Death

- 90% of Americans suffering from addiction started smoking, drinking, or using other drugs before age 18.

- Teens who engaged in binge drinking were four times more likely to have been in a physical fight in the past year than teens that did not drink.

- Six out of 10 high school students have admitted to being in a vehicle with an alcohol-impaired teen driver.

- In violent incidents recorded by the police where alcohol was a factor, about nine percent of the offenders and nearly 14 percent of the victims were under age 21.

- Women whose partners abuse alcohol are 3.6 times more likely than other women to be assaulted by their partners.

- Researchers consistently have found that men who have been drinking alcohol commit approximately one-half of all sexual assaults.

- Students usually arrive at college with an unhealthy attitude about drinking, well established at parties attended during their high-school years, and as a result, the colleges find themselves in the position of having to combat a pre-existing problem.

- Each year in the US, over 900,000 four-year college students are hit or assaulted by other students who have been drinking.

- Between 50 and 80 percent of violence on campus is alcohol-related.

- 71 percent of violent acts directed toward resident advisers were alcohol-related.

- Of students who had been victims of some type of sexual aggression—from intimidation and illegal restraint to rape—while in college, 68 percent reported their male assailants had been drinking at the time of the attack.

- 90% of all campus rapes occur when either the assailant or the victim has used alcohol.

- One in twelve college males admit to having committed acts that meet the legal definition of rape or acquaintance rape.

6.5 These Dangers Are The Tip Of The Iceberg

The dangers listed in this section are the major reasons we have not included any information that might lead teens to believe that their presence at drug and alcohol parties is OK as long as they are not using themselves. It is a simple matter for a drunk teen to assault a non-drinking one. A partygoer who tries to fool everyone by holding a fake drink might choose to replace it with a real one when pressured. This book is not an effort to help teens manage parties that feature drug and alcohol use; it is an attempt to remove the threat of drug and alcohol use from parties through adult oversight and authoritative parenting.

Furthermore, as daunting as the dangers cited above are, it is important to note that this is only a partial list. Since most teen drug and alcohol use occurs in party settings, the problem for parents becomes how to address what role parties will play in their children's lives. The ultimate goal is not to destroy your children's social lives, rather it is to make sure they are not using drugs and alcohol or spending time in the presence of others who do when they socialize.

Part 7

Conclusion

The information in this book is a lot to take in, but it all boils down to a few basic issues: Drugs and alcohol are harmful and dangerous when used by teens. Teens are most likely to consume drugs and alcohol at parties. Most parents find it difficult to manage and influence their children's social lives when it comes to parties.

If this is to change, parents have to get better at protecting their children from the harm drugs and alcohol are now understood to cause; and they must get better at limiting teens' and adolescents' access to parties where they are used. The time has come for parents to get as good at networking as their kids are; and to share the information they have about parties with each other. Please resist the urge to go it alone. Your efforts will be more rewarding if you communicate with and cooperate with other parents. Whatever differences they may have, in this matter most parents are working toward a common goal—to keep their children safe from the ravages of teen drug and alcohol use.

We laid out the bottom line in the first entry on what to do when your child is going to a party. It is *The Cardinal Rule:* When children go to parties, it is incumbent on the parents of those children to check on them at random to see if observations support their impressions of how their children spend their time. If they do not, it is also incumbent on these parents to act in such a way as to change those behaviors, and thereby change the direction of their children's lives in a positive, authoritative way.

In the beginning, especially if this effort is different from the way things were in the past, there will be some resistance on the part of the children. That is to be expected. Change of this magnitude is hard to take for most teens, and parents should expect a lot of emotion and the occasional—or frequent—threat of ruined relationships.

Those threats will beg the question, though, of the true nature of the relationship as it existed before. Children who mislead—either through outright lying or by lies of omission—about what they are doing at parties do not have an honest relationship with their parents. Parents who accept these misstatements because they fear losing a connection with their children must realize that relationships based on misinformation are not real; they are false constructs and of little or no value. True relationships are grounded in honesty, even if that truth is painful; and are made stronger by working together toward compromise and understanding. This may require some discomfort on the part of both parties, but the outcome is worth the effort.

We can get this done if parents work together; both with each other and with their children. Direct action, as we have outlined it, will be required if parents want to reduce the danger posed by teen parties that include drug and alcohol use. If we fail to act, we are consciously choosing to remain impassive in the

157

face of a direct threat to the health and safety of our children. Every increase in our understanding about the dangers of teen drug and alcohol use is a step away from being able to ignore that risk any longer and a step toward helping our teens live safe, healthy, productive lives. By learning this information, you have taken a huge stride in that direction. We encourage you to reach out to other parents and members of your community to make sure the effort does not end with you.

<u>Notes</u>

Part 1

1   *In March of 2012 in Salt Lake City:* **Teen regrets throwing party where 4 were shot** By Steve Fidel and Pat Reavy   March 19th, 2012 @ 7:06pm http://www.ksl.com/?nid=960&sid=19647689
Police said Utah teen tried to host 'Project X' party that ended in shooting By Janelle Stecklein The Salt Lake Tribune   Published March 20, 2012 11:59 pm http://www.sltrib.com/sltrib/politics/53755963-78/party-police-malan-project.html.csp

2   *In August of 2012, a 19-year-old female:* **Teen falls out of party bus onto highway; nobody on board calls 911** Published August 16, 2012 FoxNews.com   Read more: http://www.foxnews.com/us/2012/08/16/teen-falls-out-party-bus-onto-highway-nobody-on-board-calls-11/#ixzz275Sxanns

2   *On July 14, 2011, ABC News:* **Girl dies after possible alcohol poisoning at sleepover** Monday, July 11, 2011 http://abclocal.go.com/kgo/story?section=news/local/north_bay&id=8243859

2   *On March 3, 2012, a 17-year-old from Panorama City:* **Teen Dies of Alcohol Poisoning** A Panorma City teen dies from alcohol intoxication after attending a party. http://www.atvn.org/news/2012/03/teen-dies-alcohol-poisoning

4   *We will show that the majority:* Almost 75% of teen drinkers drink at parties hosted by other teens- http://www.car-accident-advice.com/statistics-of-teen-drunk-driving.html June 28, 2011

6   *Permissive parents are rarely troubled:* Positive-Parenting-Alley.com. (Retrieved September 24, 2011) Diana Baumrind's 3 Parenting Styles: Get a full understanding of the 3 archetypical parents. From http://www.positive-parenting-ally.com/parenting-styles.html

6   *Sadly, when it comes to drug and alcohol use rates:* Brigham Young University. "Teens and alcohol study: After a few drinks, parenting style kicks in." *ScienceDaily*, 25 Jun. 2010. Web. 28 Jun. 2011.

7   *At the other end of the spectrum are the authoritarian parents:* See page 6: *Permissive parents...*

7   *These parents are referred to in the BYU study:* See page 6: *Sadly, when it comes...*

7   *Authoritative parents manage:* See page 6: *Permissive parents...*

8   *Additionally, a recent study showed that children:* **[PDF] Do Parenting Styles Influence Alcohol Use and Binge Drinking** ...murphylibrary.uwlax.edu/digital/.../kusmierski-nichols-mcdonnell.pd...

8   *In late 2012, a study showed that the friends:* **Authoritative parenting can help teen friends cut drinking, smoking and drug use, researchers say.** http://consumer.healthday.com/Article.asp?AID=669431

17   *Children who have strong relationships:* Good Relationship With Parents May Prevent Teen Drinking Problems http://www.sciencedaily.com/releases/2009/04/090423180235.htm#.TjAtoHKEDd8.email

19   *As of January 1, 2011, disappointingly few states:* What parents need to know now about the new Social Host Laws http://socialhostlaw.wordpress.com/statistics/

19   *Some states, including California.* Ibid.

Part 2

32   *Familiarize yourself with your city's ordinances:* Loud and Unruly Gathering & Disturbance Advisement Violations http://www.nbpd.org/insidenbpd/services/lugo_dac.asp

Part 4

70   *In other words, it is not so much:* Teens and Peer Pressure http://www.webmd.com/parenting/teen-abuse-cough-medicine-9/peer-pressure

71	*Evidence exists that says children do not necessarily:* Peer Pressure ... An Often Misunderstood Concept http://www.extension.umn.edu/distribution/familydevelopment/00092.html
81	*As we wrote this book:* Meet Nils Pickert, the Father Who Wore a Skirt in Support of His Cross-Dressing Son http://www.thedailybeast.com/articles/2012/10/04/meet-the-dad-who-wears-skirts.html
88	*One aspect of peer pressure parents:* THE EFFECTS OF PEER PRESSURE ON TEENAGERS HTTP://WWW.LIVESTRONG.COM/ARTICLE/511686-THE-EFFECTS-OF-PEER-PRESSURE-ON-TEENAGERS/
89	*In a 2011 blog, Pat Bassett:* Bassett Blog, 2011/09: Insights from the College Front http://www.nais.org/Presidents-Corner/Bassett Blog/Lists/Posts/Post.aspx?List=a5fa8a61%2D7db4%2D4408%2D9e71%2D152670940bc3&ID=317&Web=8544a572%2D104a%2D4d86%2Dbf80%2D058334725dde
91	*One of the most powerful protective:* How to Cope With Peer Pressure http://www.wikihow.com/Cope-With-Peer-Pressure

Part 5

100-145	This section is based on information we have shared in our lecture series over the last 18 years. The following links will lead you to some highly informative sites that will allow you to explore the fascinating topic of teen brain development: http://science.education.nih.gov/Customers.nsf/HSBrain?OpenForm ; http://www.nimh.nih.gov/health/publications/the-teen-brain-still-under-construction/complete-index.shtml ; http://www.livestrong.com/article/525409-what-are-two-physical-changes-that-take-place-in-the-teen-brain/?utm_source=popslideshow&utm_medium=a1 ; http://www.livestrong.com/article/493513-teen-brain-development/ ; http://www.pbs.org/wgbh/pages/frontline/shows/teenbrain/work/adolescent.html ; http://teenbrain.drugfree.org/science/index.html ; http://teenbrain.drugfree.org/science/growth.html

Part 6

146-147	These references are listed in the order they appear on the page: *47% of 14-year-olds:* Underage Drinking http://pubs.niaaa.nih.gov/publications/AA67/AA67.htm ; *More than 90%:* Underage Drinking http://www.cdc.gov/alcohol/fact-sheets/underage-drinking.htm ; *On any given day:* http://www.ehow.com/info_7926461_alcohol-teenagers.html ; *Alcohol is the cause:* http://www.car-accident-advice.com/statistics-of-teen-drunk-driving.html ; *Over 40% of all:* Ibid. ; *There were 522 underage:* http://www.the-alcoholism-guide.org/statistics-on-teenage-drunk-driving.html#axzz1QnNcqQxG ; *In 2010, 65.2%:* 2010 Data from In-School Surveys of 8th-, 10th-, and 12th-Grade Students http://monitoringthefuture.org/data/10data.html ; *Alcohol plays a role:* . http://www.ehow.com/info_7926461_alcohol-teenagers.html ; *Almost 75% of teen drinkers:* http://www.car-accident-advice.com/statistics-of-teen-drunk-driving.html ; *Teens that binge drink:* Continuity of Binge and Harmful Drinking From Late Adolescence to Early Adulthood http://pediatrics.aappublications.org/content/114/3/714.abstract ; *Occasional heavy drinking:* Teen Drinking May Cause Irreversible Brain Damage http://www.npr.org/templates/story/story.php?storyId=122675890 ; *New studies from 2011:* University of Cincinnati. "Possible brain damage in young adult binge-drinkers revealed in new study." *ScienceDaily*, 27 Jun. 2011. Web. 28 Jun. 2011.
148-149	Listed in order of appearance on page: *One in six people:* http://www.nih.gov/news/health/dec2010/nida-14.htm ; *A 2012 article about an extensive:* Large Longitudinal Study Documents Marijuana-associated Cognitive Decline from Early Use http://journals.lww.com/neurotodayonline/Fulltext/2012/10040/Large_Longitudinal_Study_Documents.5.as ; *Low doses of THC:* http://www.nhtsa.gov/people/injury/research/job185drugs/cannabis.htm ; *Cannabis use during adolescence:* BMJ-British Medical Journal. "Cannabis use precedes the onset of psychotic symptoms in young people, study finds." *ScienceDaily*, 3 Mar. 2011. Web. 28 Jun. 2011; *Cannabis use appears:* JAMA and Archives Journals. "Psychotic illness appears to begin at younger age among those who use cannabis." *ScienceDaily*,

8 Feb. 2011. Web. 28 Jun. 2011; *New research shows that people:* Society for Neuroscience. "Human study shows greater cognitive deficits in marijuana users who start young." *ScienceDaily*, 17 Nov. 2010. Web. 28 Jun. 2011; *Recent research challenges:* American Chemical Society. "Growing Evidence Of Marijuana Smoke's Potential Dangers." *ScienceDaily*, 5 Aug. 2009. Web. 28 Jun. 2011; *A 2008 study finds that the development:* Blackwell Publishing. "Marijuana Smokers Face Rapid Lung Destruction -- As Much As 20 Years Ahead Of Tobacco Smokers." *ScienceDaily*, 27 Jan. 2008. Web. 28 Jun. 2011; *PET scans of regular marijuana users:* http://www.justthinktwice.com/factsfiction/fiction_marijuana_is_harmless.html.

150-151   Listed in order of appearance on page: *Opiates, sedatives, tranquilizers:* Drugs and the Nervous System http://www.dls.ym.edu.tw/ol_biology2/ultranet/Drugs.html ; *Six of the top 10 illicit:* http://www.nih.gov/news/health/dec2010/nida-14.htm ; *A 2011 LA Times analysis of CDC:* Drug deaths now outnumber traffic fatalities in U.S., data show; http://articles.latimes.com/2011/sep/17/local/la-me-drugs-epidemic-20110918 ; *The same LA Times article:* Ibid.; *In 2009, the CDC reported:* University of North Carolina School of Medicine. "Narcotic pain relief drug overdose deaths a national epidemic." *ScienceDaily*, 26 Apr. 2011. Web. 28 Jun. 2011; *Hospital emergency room visits:* Ibid.; *One in four 18-25 year olds:* Opioids Now Most Prescribed Class of Medications in America; http://www.sciencedaily.com/releases/2011/04/110405161906.htm; *"The scope of the problem is vast:* Ibid.; *Animal studies indicate:* Society for Neuroscience. "Morphine abuse during adolescence has multigenerational effects on brain." *ScienceDaily*, 15 Nov. 2010. Web. 28 Jun. 2011; *Adolescent brains exposed:* Rockefeller University. "Abuse Of Painkillers Can Predispose Adolescents To Lifelong Addiction." *ScienceDaily*, 11 Sep. 2008. Web. 28 Jun. 2011; *From 1998 to 2005:* http://www.webmd.com/add-adhd/news/20090824/adhd-drug-abuse-rising-among-teens.

152-153   Listed in order of appearance on page: *90% of Americans suffering:* http://www.casacolumbia.org/templates/PressReleases.aspx?articleid=641&zoneid=87 ; *Teens who engaged in binge drinking:* http://alcoholism.about.com/b/2007/06/06/binge-drinking-increases-risk-of-violence.htm June 30, 2011; *Six out of 10 high school students:* http://www.the-alcoholism-guide.org/statistics-on-teenage-drunk-driving.html#axzz1QnNcqQxG June 30, 2011; *In violent incidents recorded:* http://www.marininstitute.org/alcohol_policy/violence.htm; *Women whose partners:* Ibid.; *Researchers consistently have found:* http://www.athealth.com/Practitioner/ceduc/alc_assault.html June 30, 2011; *Students usually arrive at college:* http://www.edweek.org/ew/articles/2000/07/12/42weeks.h19.html?qs=College+Drinking June 30, 2011; *Each year in the US, over 900,000:* http://www.higheredcenter.org/files/product/secondary-effects.txt June 30, 2011; *Between 50 and 80 percent:* Ibid.; *71 percent of violent acts:* Ibid.; *Of students who had been victims:* Ibid.; *90% of all campus rapes:* http://apps.carleton.edu/campus/wellness/physical_health/alcohol/sex/ June 30, 2011; *One in twelve college males:* Ibid.

Where's The Party?
Lessons in Drug Prevention: Handbook Three
The How-To Party Protocol Book for Parents and Teens
First Edition

To order any of our products or services, please visit:
www.milestogodrugeducation.com
Kelly Townsend, M.S. & Jonathan Scott

Made in the USA
Charleston, SC
25 November 2016